P9-EDG-780

To David,

VISIONARY
BUSINESS

Enjoy!

Marc Allen

VISIÖNARY
BUSINESS

AN ENTREPRENEUR'S GUIDE
TO SUCCESS

MARC ALLEN

NEW WORLD LIBRARY
NOVATO, CALIFORNIA

New World Library
14 Pamaron Way
Novato, California 94949
© 1995 Marc Allen

Cover design: Nita Ybarra Design
Editorial: Gina Misiroglu
Text design: Tori Hernandez

All rights reserved. This book may not be reproduced in whole or in part without written permission from the publisher, except by a reviewer who may quote brief passages in a review; nor may any part of this book be reproduced, stored in a retrieval system, or transmitted in any form or by any means electronic, mechanical, photocopying, recording, or other, without written permission from the publisher.

Library of Congress Cataloging-in-Publication Data

Allen, Mark, 1946–

Visionary Business: an entrepreneur's guide to success / Marc Allen.

p. cm.

ISBN 1-880032-46-5 (alk. paper)

1. Success in business. 2. Industrial management. I. Title.

HF5386.A535 1996   95-33675

658.1'1— dc20   CIP

First printing, December, 1995
Printed in the U.S.A. on acid-free paper
ISBN 1-880032-46-5
Distributed to the trade by Publishers Group West
10 9 8 7 6 5 4 3 2 1

Dedicated to all those who dare to dream, and all those who have the knowledge, generosity, and heart to support others in reaching their dreams.

"Keep away from people who try to belittle your ambitions. Small people always do that, but the really great make you feel that you, too, can somehow become great."

— Mark Twain

Contents

INTRODUCTION

THIS IS A FICTIONALIZED ACCOUNT of a true story. There really was a Bernie, the central prophet in this tale of wisdom, though somewhere in the telling of the story, his character grew and merged with several other people I have been fortunate enough to know, including a wonderful man named Michael Bliss, who was ninety years young when I met him, still teaching piano and cello, and inspiring all who came around to his little house in Malibu, California.

I have not adhered very closely to actual historical facts, but have focused more on the principles and the keys of visionary business — the keys that have been given to me, one by one, over the past twenty years or so from a variety of sources.

It is my fervent wish that this book can significantly help a number of people to improve their businesses and the quality of their lives — and, by doing so, make this world a better place for all. For that is the ultimate goal of a visionary business: to transform the world, by doing what we love to do, into an ecologically sustainable environment, with peace and plenty for all God's creatures.

VISIONARY
BUSINESS

KEY ONE

\\\\\\\\/

Imagine your ideal scene.

SEVERAL YEARS AGO, with the help of a few friends, I started my own business. We were like most founders of small businesses: full of dreams, but short of concrete business experience; full of ideas, but seriously short of cash. We were overworked and underpaid. We were overwhelmed much of the time, and seriously undercapitalized.

We had a great many vague ideals, but had never written a concrete mission statement. We had high hopes, but had never written a business plan.

We set up a small office, and furnished it with the bare necessities to conduct business. All three of us continued to work at other jobs, part-time, and poured as much cash as we could into the business. All of our savings (which wasn't much — a few thousand dollars) went into the company. A few friends and relatives invested, and a few others loaned us money. But the money always went quickly, and we were continually strapped for cash.

For those who invested, we promised a share of ownership in the company. They would become stockholders, and officially own some portion of something, as soon as we got around to incorporating. But month after month passed, and we never got around to setting up a corporation. We were too swept up in the vast number of never-ending daily details that had to be handled to be able to step back and do any long-term planning.

One of our first employees quit; he felt there was too much stress in the company, and too little security. He didn't want to worry about whether his paycheck would be good or not every pay period. I couldn't blame him; he wasn't getting paid enough to deal with the level of anxiety in the company. None of us were, but at least those of us who were the owners had the possibility of having something of value in a distant, vaguely fantasized future.

My other job was flexible free-lance work, so I was able to work nearly full-time at the office. I always tried to get out of the office in the morning and again in the afternoon for at least a brief walk. I usually found some kind of errand that needed to be run, or sometimes I would just walk around the block. I needed to get out of the confined space of that office to do some thinking, to clear my head of the myriad details that threatened to overwhelm me at times.

One morning, as I left the office, I saw an old man sitting on a bench across the street. He caught my eye because he was sitting motionlessly, gazing into space ... an old man, far away. When I returned from my errands, he was sitting in exactly the same position. Apparently, he hadn't moved a muscle in at least half an hour. He was looking in the general direction of our office, but his gaze seemed way beyond any specific focus.

His eyes and facial expression reminded me of something, but I couldn't remember what. It was quiet, reflective; there was a touch of sadness, but then there was a touch of humor, too. Then I remembered where I had seen those eyes, and that expression: on the Yoda doll on my dresser — the Jedi master from the *Star Wars* movies. ...

I saw him a few times after that, always sitting in the same position. I don't think I ever saw him move. He was striking in his silence and stillness.

Then one day he crossed the street and walked in the door of our little office. I seem to recall it was a beautiful spring day, though I hadn't paid much attention to it. My attention had been on the crisis of the day. I don't even remember now what the particular crisis had been — each day had its own problems. About all we were doing was crisis management: dealing with one demanding situation after another.

He breezed in the door, uninvited and certainly unexpected. He was wearing a brown old-man suit, with brown shoes — quite conservative dress. Nobody knew who he was. He stood there, hands in his pockets, and carefully looked around the office. He looked as if he almost expected us to welcome him, as if he had an appointment with someone.

He had sharp features, and his white wavy hair was combed straight back, held into place with a substantial quantity of gel or grease. His skin was stretched taut over his face; he was old, but it was impossible to tell his age. At first it seemed like he didn't have a wrinkle on his face, but as he turned into the light, I could see his delicate skin was covered with fine lines.

I walked over to him. "Can I help you?" I said.

"I don't know," he said, with a slight smile. "Maybe, maybe not." He held out his hand. "My name's Bernie."

I shook his hand; his fingers were long and delicate and cool. There was something warm and friendly about the old guy; something that immediately put me at ease.

"I'm Marc."

"Nice little business you've got here."

"Well, it's just a beginning, I hope."

"How long have you been in business?"

"Oh, we've had the office about six months, though we've been working on it for over a year now."

"I like the way you've furnished the office."

He said it with a slight smile; I didn't know if he was kidding or not. The office furniture was a hodge-podge of the cheapest stuff we could find at flea markets and garage sales, with a few leftovers from our apartments thrown in.

"It's the low-cost way to go," I said.

"That's what I like about it," he said. "I've seen start-up companies who have put all their money into the furniture. I invested in a company awhile ago, in fact, and the two owners went out and bought Mercedes automobiles and custom-built oak desks and artwork for the walls. I couldn't believe it! They even had custom-built bookcases. I told them they needed to spend their money on their business, not on their furniture. They promised me they'd be fine — and they went bankrupt before the year was out. They didn't invest in the future."

He paused and looked around the office.

"As a start-up, you've got to spend wisely. Only spend money on the things that'll make that money grow. And don't buy a Mercedes until you can well afford it."

His story piqued my interest. I didn't know what to say; there was a pause in the conversation that felt awkward to me. He simply looked at me, carefully, with that slight smile of his. I felt as if he was assessing something; I had no idea what.

"Are you people looking for an investor?" He said it casually, giving it no more importance than if he was asking me for the time of day.

"Well . . . we certainly are in need of some capital."

"Do you have a business plan?"

"Ah . . . no, not really. Lots of ideas, and plans, but nothing really concrete on paper, yet. . . ."

I suddenly became aware that we were both standing, somewhat awkwardly, near the doorway. At least I felt awkward. Bernie seemed supremely comfortable, with his hands in his pockets.

"Would you like some coffee, or something?" I said. "Would you like to sit down?"

"Sure, that would be fine."

After a brief tour of the office — it certainly didn't take long to tour our entire operation — we got some coffee and sat in my little office in the back. Bernie liked his coffee loaded with milk and sugar. As he stirred it in, I noticed the cuff links he sported: large one-ounce gold coins. And his tie tack was made out of one of the biggest gold nuggets I had ever seen.

He didn't waste time getting down to business. "You need a plan," he said. "I might invest; I might not. You don't know me from Adam — I could be a weirdo off the street who's conning you for a free cup of coffee." He said it with his enigmatic smile. He could have been speaking the truth — I had no idea.

"But it doesn't matter. If all I do is encourage you to get started on a plan, my little visit here would have been worth your time. You need a solid, well-written business plan before any investor will take you seriously. Every company needs a business plan, whether they need investors or not. A business without a plan is like a ship without a course. You just wander around aimlessly, without reaching any destination, because you haven't charted out the course necessary to get anywhere. You haven't even determined your destination.

"Your plan doesn't have to be long and involved; it doesn't have to be complex. But it has to be clear, to you and to anyone else who's interested. And it has to be in writing, of course. Start with a brief, concise mission statement. Make it as idealistic as you can, as grand as you want. Then describe your business: what it is, what you do as a company. Describe clearly where you're at, as of today. Tell us who are involved, and what you do. Then tell us where you want to be in a year, two years, and five years — and show us your map for getting there.

"First do it as simply as possible — and as briefly as possible — in words; then show us with numbers. Show us your cash flow projections for the next five years. It should be clear how much capital you're going to need, what you're going to do with it, and what results you predict."

"Okay," I said. I grabbed a note pad and started

making some notes. This guy may have been a wacko, but he was giving some very good advice.

"But I want to suggest doing one thing first, even before you do your plan — a great exercise that will help you with your plan, among other things. How many people work here?"

"A total of five. Plus a part-time bookkeeper."

"How many of you are owners?"

"Three of us started the company."

"The other two are paid employees?"

"Right. The owners don't draw anything out of the company yet."

"How are you set up? A partnership?"

I hesitated before answering. "Yes, though we haven't really finalized the agreement."

Bernie looked at me oddly, coldly. His eyes were a pale gray, almost luminescent. "Partnerships don't work," he said flatly.

"What do you mean?" I said. "There have been lots of successful partnerships."

"Name two."

I laughed. I was certain there were many, many successful partnerships in the world — but I couldn't think of any at the moment. Bernie seemed to enjoy watching me squirm.

"What about law firms, and accounting firms?" I said. "Aren't they partnerships?"

"Oh, there are a lot of successful businesses organized as partnerships," Bernie said, completely contradicting himself. "But they don't operate as partnerships."

He left it there, as if it should be obvious to me. It wasn't.

"What do you mean?" I said.

"A partnership usually means two or more people are responsible, ultimately, for the company, right? For the executive decisions. And over time, two or more people will never agree on everything. There are always disagreements; there will always be conflict. Even if the business is organized as a partnership, legally, one person has to be the president. One person has to make the final decisions. One person has to be responsible for the success or failure of the business."

I didn't know if I agreed with his sweeping generalizations.

"Why?" I asked.

"Because partnerships don't work." He smiled; he seemed on the verge of laughter. His smugness was a little irritating. So was his logic.

"Look — how often has it happened in your company that one of the partners assumes the other is responsible for something, only to find that the other one has assumed someone else is responsible — and something important has not been taken care of? Has that ever happened to you?"

I had to admit it had, more than once.

"That's the nature of partnerships," he said. "No one is fully responsible for the whole picture.

So things get neglected. The ball gets dropped, because no one person is responsible for that ball being carried the whole distance. And another thing that always happens — *always* happens — is that one partner will feel they're putting in more time, and energy, and maybe even money, than another partner. There's never an equal balance — that's impossible to achieve. One always feels they're carrying a greater load than the other."

I had to admit I'd had those feelings as well.

"I suggest you form a corporation, and put one person in charge. Or if it seems premature to form a corporation, at least choose someone to be president. Some people resist this, saying it's hierarchical, but I've found, in my experience, it's practical. It's efficient. It works. And it doesn't necessarily have to be hierarchical. The president doesn't necessarily have to be the boss, and tell everyone else what to do. But one person has to carry the vision of success, and has to be responsible for realizing that vision. The others can be on the Board of Directors; they can head different departments, different divisions that reflect their particular area of expertise — but the buck has got to stop somewhere, with one person. If you want to be egalitarian, or whatever you want to call it, or if you have two strong leaders, you could even rotate the leadership role. But at every moment, one person has to be in charge."

"I can see your point."

"Good. Now here's the exercise I'd suggest you do, before you do your business plan — and it may help you determine who's going to be president, if it isn't already obvious. It'll certainly help you with your business plan:

"Have everybody in the company sit down — or at least have the owners sit down, if the employees are uncomfortable doing this — and everybody write down, on paper, *exactly what they want to be doing five years from now.* Assume that your business has grown according to plan — in fact assume that everything has gone fantastically well, and you have had success beyond your wildest dreams — then ask yourself what you'd like to be doing. What is your *ideal scene?* What if money were no object, what if you could have exactly the kind of life you wanted, what would it be? Put it in writing, and read it to each other. Do this before you begin your business plan. You'll be in for some revelations."

He finished his coffee. We exchanged cards, and he left. I still had no idea what to think of him. He could have been an old man living in a fantasy world, for all I knew. But he had a business card, and it read:

UIC
Universal Investment Corporation

That sounded promising. An address and phone number followed; the address looked like it was a room or suite in a hotel.

We did the exercise Bernie suggested, which we dubbed the "ideal scene process." All five of us in our little company sat down and described, on paper, the kind of life we wanted to be living five years in the future, assuming everything had gone as well as we could imagine.

Bernie was right: We were in for some revelations. I was the only one of the three owners who even wanted to be running the business five years in the future. The other two wanted to use the business as a springboard to launch them into other creative careers. If we hadn't have done that process, we wouldn't have understood that so clearly. It helped us put not only the future but the present into a clearer perspective. I became the president of the company, focusing on new product development; the other two became vice-presidents in charge of marketing and operations respectively.

It became my responsibility to write the business plan — with a lot of help from my friends, of course.

SUMMARY

✳ A start-up company should only spend money on the things that will make that money grow.

✳ Every company needs a business plan, whether they need investors or not. A business without a plan is like a ship without a course.

✳ Business plans don't have to be long and involved, but they have to be in writing and clear, to you and to anyone else who reads it. First describe your business and your present circumstances; then describe where you want to be in a year, two years, and five years — and present a map for getting there. First do it as simply as possible in words, then with numbers.

✳ Start your business plan with a brief, concise mission statement. Make it as idealistic as you can, as grand as you want. A mission statement helps the company retain its focus and can be crucial in determining the company's direction and even its level of success.

✳ Remember that partnerships work only in unique situations; most businesses that operate as partnerships run into difficulties. One person has to be completely responsible for the success or failure of the business.

❋ Be sure the owners of the business — and, ideally, all of the employees as well — write their "ideal scenes" down on paper, and compare notes: What do you want to be doing five years from now, assuming that your business has grown according to plan — in fact assume that everything has gone fantastically well, and you have had success beyond your wildest dreams. What would your life look like? What would you be doing? Where would you live? What would a typical day look like? This simple exercise is a powerful visionary tool.

Key Two

\\||/

*Write your business plan as a clear
and concrete visualization.*

WRITING THE BUSINESS PLAN was not an easy task. The financial projections were especially difficult; I needed a great deal of assistance from a great many people to make realistic projections. It took far more time than I thought it would.

Bernie had told me to make monthly projections for the first year or two, then quarterly projections for the rest. I had to imagine every conceivable expense, as accurately as possible. Finances were never my strong point; making all those projections was no fun at all. I continually had the feeling that I was forgetting something important, something that would change everything. And I kept discovering new expenses, and they seemed exorbitant and overwhelming. Taxes

— federal, state, county, and sales taxes. All the additional things added to payroll — the list seemed endless. Insurance — we needed far more than we had. Accounting. Legal advice.

The projections for income were nerve-wracking as well: Who had any idea what our income would be five years in the future? Or one year? Or six months? I was pulling projections out of the clear blue sky, and fearing I was being far too optimistic. Yet, if I was less optimistic, I couldn't see a way to become profitable. It was a dilemma that kept me awake at night.

It took over three long months to finally complete it. I hadn't heard a word from Bernie. I called him and got an answering machine. I left a message, and Bernie got back to me the next day. He told me to bring the business plan and meet him at his office. It felt like a special day — I even put on a sports coat and tie for the occasion.

Bernie's "office" turned out to be a suite in a hotel on the mezzanine floor that had a large balcony in front of his door that looked out over the lobby. He said he liked to have his office in a hotel because they had room service. We sat on large stuffed chairs on the balcony and had lunch delivered to us. Bernie had a ham sandwich on white bread, and coffee with a heavy dose of milk and sugar.

I felt quite a bit of trepidation as I handed him

the business plan. According to our cash flow projections, we were going to need quite an infusion of capital — quite soon — if we were going to reach our goals. Or even if we were going to stay in business. Without some outside financing, the future looked pretty bleak.

He read through it quickly, skimming through most parts of it. He gave the financial pages a bit more of a thorough reading, though he seemed to just glance over most of the specifics and focus more intently on a few select numbers. I sat fidgeting as he read in silence.

"It's a good start," he said finally, still staring at the numbers. "You've done your homework."

I smiled, and swelled a bit with pride.

"But I want you to rewrite it."

My swelling quickly diminished. "What's wrong with it?" I asked.

"Nothing's terribly wrong — but you don't have enough contingencies built in. Things rarely happen as we project them to happen. There are always contingencies, unexpected developments, unforeseen problems — and they usually cost money.

"I have a rule of thumb: Everything in a start-up business will take twice as long and cost twice as much as you expect. This may sound pessimistic, but it's based on experience. The single biggest problem small start-up companies face is that they project they need x number of dollars, and they raise *x* number of dollars, and then they spend it and still need more of a cash infusion. But their investors are stretched to the limit, or they've invested all they intend to invest because the people in the company have blown their credibility by not performing as they said they would. I've seen so many companies collapse that were 90 percent there, so close to making it, but they just couldn't raise that last 10 percent of capital they needed. The well was dry. They had lost the trust of their investors.

"Make sure your plan is realistic. Make sure you're asking for plenty of capital, enough to cover every imaginable contingency. And at the bottom of your expense pages, add another 15 percent or so for contingencies — unforeseen expenses. Okay?"

"Okay." I was not too happy at the thought of rewriting the plan, and I couldn't help but feel that, if we did as Bernie suggested, we might be in need of so much money that we would never find anyone with the resources to invest that much.

And there was another fear, one that had kept me awake more than a few nights: If we really did need twice as much as we were projecting, which was certainly a possibility, how could we make enough of a profit that the investors would get some kind of reasonable return on investment? It was a very real dilemma, one I had wrestled with. Bernie seemed to read my mind.

"Don't worry about asking for what might seem like a lot of money. And don't worry, at this point, about return on investment. Let your investors deal with that. You need to create a document you can work with.

"A well-written business plan is far more than a tool for raising money. This plan is your map, your visualization of the future." He held it up dramatically. I couldn't help smiling as he said "visualization" — it seemed an uncharacteristic word for an old man in a brown suit.

"The clearer, the more concrete, the visualization, the greater the chance of achieving it. You need a plan that not only makes sense financially, but that feels achievable, on a gut level. You need a plan that is so clear and strong that it seeps deeply into your subconscious mind, and sets the whole universe in motion to bring about the results you desire.

"Your plan has to be strong enough to overcome every possible hurdle and obstacle, external and internal — external problems like lack of capital, competition, changes in the marketplace and economy, as well as your own internal obstacles of fear, doubt, lack of self-esteem or self-respect, lack of experience and knowledge, and so on."

Bernie seemed positively radiant. He looked about twenty years younger, filled with vitality, as he spoke.

"This plan is powerful! Because it's capable of

setting your powerful subconscious mind in motion!

"Once you have a clear plan, nothing can stop you — except yourself, or unless you're violating some basic universal laws, laws apparent to any sensible person, anyone with some ethics, or any kind of religious background.

"Once you have a clear plan, you turn your desire for success into an *intention.* Once you have the intention to succeed, 90 percent of your perceived obstacles will dissolve, and you will have the tools to deal with the other 10 percent as they come up. In fact, those obstacles will become your opportunities.

"Don't forget that: Turn your desires into intentions; turn your obstacles and problems into opportunities. I have a big sign over my desk that reads: *For every adversity, there's an equal or greater opportunity.* Another way to say it is a popular cliché — but it's one of our best clichés, because it's true: *Where there's a will, there's a way.*"

He gave me that same look he'd given me the day we met — as if he was assessing something within me.

"I don't think you've got anything to worry about," he said, somewhat ambiguously. "Let's call room service and have some dessert. Or at least some more coffee."

Summary

- ❋ Write a clear and concrete business plan. Make monthly projections for the first year or two, then quarterly projections for the rest.

- ❋ Build contingencies into your plan. Try to imagine every possible expense, then total all expenses and add another 15 percent or so to that total for contingencies — unforeseen expenses.

- ❋ Remember this rule of thumb: Everything in a start-up business will take twice as long and cost twice as much as you expect. Be sure to plan to have enough resources to overcome delays in time and unexpected expenses.

- ❋ A well-written business plan is far more than a tool for raising money: It is your map, your visualization of the future. The clearer, the more concrete the visualization, the greater your chance of achieving it.

- ❋ Your plan has to be strong enough to overcome every possible hurdle and obstacle, external and internal. A business plan is powerful, because it sets in motion your powerful sub-conscious mind.

✳ A well-written business plan turns your desire for success into an *intention*. Once you have the intention to succeed, 90 percent of your perceived obstacles will dissolve, and you will have the tools to deal with the other 10 percent as they come up.

✳ Turn your desires into intentions; turn your obstacles and problems into opportunities. *For every adversity, there is an equal or greater opportunity*. Another way to phrase this has been a part of our language for a long time: Where there's a will, there's a way.

KEY THREE

Discover your higher purpose.

ERNIE'S LITTLE TALK really surprised me. Here was this old man, by almost anyone's standards — he was certainly over seventy — talking about visualization, and your subconscious mind. But his words were inspiring — and his office suite proved he had attained some degree of success. I made some notes after our meeting, so I'd remember his words.

I went back to work on the business plan and wrestled with it until I felt good about it. I could see that Bernie was certainly right in one respect: I grew to understand more deeply how the plan was our visualization of the possible future. The first exercise he had suggested to us, the "ideal scene process," was a fantasy, although it was a valuable stretching of the imagination. Working on the business plan, however, brought that fantasy down into concrete terms. As I completed the revision of it, I felt that I was somehow nearly halfway toward achieving it — and that I had already completed the most difficult part, or at least the most essential part. For without a vision of the future, there is no future.

Every successful business is based on a vision. Someone has first clearly imagined the development and growth of that business, far before that growth occurred in physical reality. I saw more clearly what Bernie had been telling me: What begins as a dream, a fantasy, an "ideal scene," must be translated into a solid business plan, with specific numbers. This sets in motion the forces that can bring the fantasy into concrete reality.

I went to see Bernie again a few weeks later, armed with a substantially revised plan. I was nervous about it; we were asking for a great deal more money than before. But, given that amount of investment, the plan felt solid. There were enough reserves for any contingencies I could imagine. At least, I hoped that was true. But then I've always been an optimist — though one with, at times, severe self-doubts.

Bernie met me at the door of his suite, wearing the same suit as before, apparently, with the same gold cuff links and tie tack. We sat on the balcony in the same seats, and he ordered his ham sandwich on white bread and coffee with lots of milk and sugar.

He glanced through the plan quickly, as he had before. He seemed to know exactly what he was looking for — he'd skim over most of it, then stop and focus carefully on certain information.

"This is much better. Hmmmm...."

I felt an uncomfortable degree of anxiety. I was sweating. If he invested in us, we could finally have some money to develop new products and to promote them in the way they should be promoted. We would be able to pay off our debts, without having to constantly field anxious phone calls about overdue bills. And we would finally be able to pay ourselves a regular salary, week after week. I could quit my other part-time job, and focus on the business.

Bernie gave me one of his penetrating looks. He was assessing something again, something within me.

"What's your main purpose in all this?" he asked me.

"My main purpose?" I sensed a trick question. I had to tread carefully.

"In doing this plan, in raising this money — hopefully — you have some kind of purpose. What is it? Do you want to make a ton of money? Do you want to retire in a mansion? Do you want to create great value for the stockholders? Be honest, now."

I had no other choice. I couldn't face his gaze

and lie to him. But he was asking a very difficult question. "When I try to put my main purpose into words," I said, "it comes out sounding pretty hackneyed, or something. But I'd like to help people. I'd like to do something significant, something meaningful ... something that makes a valuable contribution to people and maybe even helps the world in some way be a better place to live in...."

I paused, searching for words. Bernie was in no hurry to speak. There was a silence.

"That's as close as I can come to defining a purpose at the moment, I guess." It felt like it wasn't a very good statement of purpose. I'd forgotten what we had put in our mission statement at the front of the plan. But Bernie didn't seem too disappointed.

"Good," he said, "you're on the right track. You have to have a higher purpose than making money in a business. If you have a higher purpose, you marshall all kinds of forces behind you and within you that support you in your goal. You get support from all kinds of places — some that you plan on, some that you can't possibly plan on. It's almost mystical — I think it *is* mystical — I've seen it happen over and over. If your purpose is just making money, you wither and die. You might even be successful, to some degree, but you're still unfulfilled, and you wither and die. I've seen that happen over and over, too.

"Money is essential in business, but it's secondary. Money is the lifeblood of the business, but the business has to have a higher purpose to survive and thrive.

"There are a lot of people who believe that the purpose of a business is to make money. I feel sorry for them. They have such a tough row to hoe. You sense it all the time, from the little businesses that'll do anything to make a buck to all the big businesses whose leaders are always using phrases like 'maximizing shareholder value.' It leads to stupid business decisions that can have disastrous results for both the company and the environment.

"That kind of thinking, to me, is as stupid as believing that the purpose of our lives here on earth is to keep blood pumping through our bodies. Sure, we have to have blood pumping through our bodies in order to be alive, but our purpose in life is something far more significant, far greater."

He went back to looking at the plan, flipping through it casually, glancing at random at different pages. It was nerve-wracking. I knew he was giving me valuable advice, but it was hard to focus on it.

"Each of us is different," he said, looking back at me again, and stressing his words so that I had no choice but to listen, "and each of us has a unique purpose for living. And in order to accomplish that purpose, each of us has been given some unique talents and abilities. There is something you can do, and something I can do, that no one else can do in quite the same way. We all have these natural gifts. Sometimes it's difficult for us to discover what they are — and sometimes it's because it's so obvious; it's so easy for us to perform in a certain way that we take it for granted and don't realize what a gift it is.

"Each of us should spend some time — however much time is necessary, and whenever necessary — to reflect on our purpose, and discover our purpose. Most true purposes involve service of some kind, some form of love, some form of positive contribution to humanity or to the planet. We each need to discover our purpose, in order to be truly successful.

"Our purpose is a sacred thing. I don't think it's something we should go around advertising. I don't even think — and this is just my opinion, of course — but I don't think we should even tell anyone else what our purpose is, except maybe our best friend, or our business partner, or our marriage partner. We should discover our purpose ourselves, and live it. Then, and only then, are we fulfilled in life."

There was a moment of silence.

"Do you know what I'm talking about?"

I nodded, but found no words to say. He gave me that look again.

"I'll roll the dice with you," he said.

Summary

＊ A well-written business plan brings the fantasy of your "ideal scene" down into concrete terms. Your plan is your most essential step, because it contains your vision of the future.

＊ Every successful business is based on a vision. Someone has first clearly imagined the development and growth of that business, far before that growth occurred in physical reality.

＊ You have to have a higher purpose than making money in a business. If you have a higher purpose, you marshall all kinds of forces behind you and within you that support you in your goal.

＊ You have a unique purpose for living, and you have been given unique talents and abilities to accomplish that purpose. You need to reflect on your purpose, and discover it, in order to be truly successful. True success always involves personal fulfillment of some kind, and you are fulfilled only by working and living in harmony with your purpose in life.

KEY FOUR

\||/

See the benefits within adversity,
and keep picturing success.

I WENT BACK TO THE OFFICE in a state of shock, mingled with euphoria. Bernie had said he would talk to his lawyer and call us in a few days and "firm up the details."

For some reason I had thought that, before he made his decision, he would carefully study every aspect of the business plan, and question us about the nature of our business, and about our projections and expenses. I had imagined him challenging our numbers, questioning what we assumed we would need to spend on salaries, or on other expenses — manufacturing, or promotion, or taxes. There was none of that. He made his decision much faster than I had expected.

A few days later, he called and set up another meeting. "We'll go over the terms," he said, "and if everything is okay with you, I'll get the papers drawn up. You're going to have to set up a corporation. Do you have a lawyer?"

"Well, not really — but we can get one," I said.

"Don't worry about it. I'll have my lawyer draw it up. It won't cost that much — it's boiler-plate stuff."

"Okay." I was assuming the cost to incorporate would come out of his investment — we certainly didn't have it in the bank. We had, as usual, nothing at all in the bank.

"Oh, the only other thing I need is a list of your assets. All three owners will have to pledge your assets as collateral."

"Bernie, we have very few assets."

"Any of you own a house?"

"No."

"Well, just list whatever you have, and we'll have to make do with that."

I didn't want him to get any kind of wrong impression.

"I've got to warn you, Bernie — it's not much."

"Don't worry about it — but draw up a list anyway."

"Okay..."

The ritual of our next meeting was exactly the same as the last two. I wondered if Bernie ever tired of ham on white bread. He didn't eat that much of it though, I noticed. He didn't even finish half of it.

"I came across a great new business plan the other day," Bernie said, flashing his golden cuff links. "It's a company that turns garbage into energy — they take garbage and run it through this process and turn it into little blocks that burn like coal, only cleaner. What a great business! Can you imagine? They pay *you* for your raw materials!"

He said it with the enthusiasm of a child. He seemed to be immensely enjoying what he was doing.

"The owners of the company asked me if I planned to retire," he said, smiling broadly, "What a question! I don't believe in retirement. Retiring sounds like something they do to old horses, sending them to pasture. I'll never retire.

"I invest in quite a few companies, businesses of all kinds. That's what I love to do. And I'll tell you, the people I've invested in who have failed all really love me, you know? And some of those that get successful end up resenting me."

At the time I didn't know what he meant. Later on, I understood.

"I wish you great success," Bernie went on, "and I sure hope you don't end up resenting me. Because here's what I'm prepared to offer you: I'll loan you the money you need for the first nine months. After that, you may need additional capital, according to your plan. I'll introduce you to my banker, and perhaps the bank can take over financing at that point. We want to get you a line of credit with a bank as soon as possible.

"The loan will be a seven-year note; you pay interest only for the first year — or maybe two, if you need to. Interest will be three points above prime. I'll have an option in the deal as well — an option to exchange 25 percent of the amount of the note you owe for 25 percent ownership of the company. I can exercise the option any time during the next three years; after three years, it expires. Okay?"

I felt in no position to argue with him. He was holding all the cards. Later on I realized that by taking 25 percent of the principal off the note in exchange for a 25 percent equity position in the company, he was in effect valuing the company to equal the amount of his loan — and that was, at the time, a generous valuation, several times the gross sales for that year.

"Oh, one more thing," Bernie said, almost as if he had nearly forgotten it. "Did you bring a list of your collateral?"

I reluctantly handed it to him.

"You weren't kidding when you said you had no collateral," he said. There was a smile in his voice, though — he seemed to think our financial situation was humorous. And he seemed impressed, too, that we were honest and made no attempt to inflate our assets — but then, it's hard to inflate something that's non-existent.

"I'll have my lawyer set up a corporation. You'll need to protect all these assets, after all." This was Bernie's idea of a joke. "He'll call you. It won't take long to set up."

I met Bernie a short time later at the office of his lawyer, a man about Bernie's age — whatever that was — who had a great capacity for story-telling. He and Bernie both regaled me with stories for well over an hour. Neither seemed in any hurry to get to the point.

Their stories were fascinating — they had a great many years of experience between them. They both obviously loved what they were doing, and found great pleasure in entertaining a new-comer to the business world.

The most memorable story Bernie's lawyer told was about an old man from India who had come into his office. He was shabbily dressed; he looked like one of the street people that seemed to be pro-liferating in the neighborhood. He asked the lawyer to set up a corporation for him, and gave him a battered, greasy check for the legal work. The lawyer thought he was a bum living out a fanta-sy, and he gave the check to one of his assistants to see if by any chance it was good. The manager of the bank said it was definitely good; in fact the man had a *fifty million dollar* personal line of credit with the bank. It turned out the old man imported vast quantities of American-grown food to India, buying by the railroad car load. Though he chose to dress like a street person, he was an extremely wealthy individual.

Bernie told a memorable story, too: "I used to own a hotel in Havana, back in the fifties," he said. "As I was driving to work one day, there was a skirmish in the street, right in front of me. As I drove by, I could see that the police had surrounded a young supporter of Castro, and were apprehending him. I was so close to that kid I could see his eyes, clearly. And I saw incredible determination and commitment. And I realized Castro was going to win; Batiste could not survive against that kind of fierce support.

"I sold the hotel, immediately. And I told the other owners to sell, too. But they all said the same thing. 'No, Castro will never take over. And even if he does, he has promised us he'll leave the hotels alone.' I sold and left town. Within a year, all those owners had lost everything."

There was a lesson in that story, I thought: *Trust your instincts.*

When they finally finished their storytelling, Bernie's lawyer put his hand on the pile of legal documents.

"Okay — let's get down to business." He looked at me in depth, as if he were sizing me up in the same way Bernie often did. "Bernie's been very good to us over the years...."

I wasn't sure what he meant by that, exactly. I

figured it probably meant he worked with a pool of investors, including his lawyer.

"He has an eye for talent," he said, looking at me. I had a feeling he was not very impressed by me; I felt inexperienced and young.

The next hour or so was spent going over the documents — loan papers and articles of incorporation. There were six stockholders in our newly formed corporation: the three investors we had promised some form of equity, and the three founders. Bernie had worked out a formula, giving what seemed like a fair amount of stock to everyone, relative to their particular contribution. As we finished signing all the various documents, Bernie leaned back in his chair, and gazed wistfully into the unknown.

"Never forget: I'm investing in *you.* I'm not investing in your business plan, or your corporation. You can have the greatest plan in the world, you can have the best-capitalized corporation in the world, but if you don't have good people running it, you have no future.

"I'm investing in your vision and integrity and good sense. It's up to you to keep the vision of the company so clear that everyone you work with can feel it — and it has to be a vision of growth and success. You've got to be able to clearly imagine how your company can quickly become profitable, and steadily grow, increasing those profits, just as you've outlined in your five-year plan.

"It's up to you to be able to see every problem as an opportunity. Never forget this: *For every adversity, there is an equal or greater benefit.* That, in one sentence, is a key to visionary business. Life is always filled with problems, but it's filled with opportunities as well. Learn to spot the opportunities that are inherent in every problem."

He stopped for a moment, then said, "I hope you don't mind me sitting here spouting all this advice."

"No, not at all," I said. I had been listening carefully, trying to remember as much as possible.

"Here's maybe the single best piece of advice I can give you: Spend some time in solitude, every day if you can. Spend some time reviewing your goals, keeping your dreams fresh in your mind. Focus on your plan — both on the long-term goals and on the very next step in front of you toward your next goal. Always keep moving forward.

"Don't dwell on any pictures of failure. Keep picturing success. I firmly believe that no company should *ever* go into bankruptcy — it's a failure of the vision of the leaders of the company. If you can't imagine failure and bankruptcy, you can't possibly fail.

"There are no bad businesses, there are only poor managers. A good manager can take *any* kind of business and turn it around and make it successful. A poor manager can take any kind of business and run it into the ground. I've seen it over and over. So have you, if you stop to think about it."

I thought about it. I had seen it.

"Your success may take a different route than you planned — that happens all the time. The trick is to make a clear plan, a clear path to success, but then to be flexible enough to change your plans continually as new problems and obstacles and opportunities arise. Your business might look totally different in five years than you imagine it will look. That's okay. You have to be flexible, and willing to do whatever it takes to reach your goals. We're in a changing universe; if we learn to adapt to those changes, we can always reach our goals, somehow. If we resist those changes, we are fighting against the universe, and we'll always lose that battle."

Bernie's lawyer was obviously enjoying his spiel. He smiled and nodded, silently cheering Bernie on. He obviously loved Bernie, and enjoyed his little speeches as much as I did.

"It's really exciting to me every time we set up a new corporation," Bernie said. "The corporation is a great invention, when you think about it — as great an invention as compound interest, which was a *brilliant* invention. The corporation is its own legal entity; it's an individual, just like you and me. It grows like you and me. It goes through the stages of infancy, youth, and maturity. It takes on its own personality — reflecting in an almost mystical way its leaders, but it has a life of its own, separate from its owners or employees or anyone else.

"Every corporation, like every individual, has the capability to be infinitely creative. There are endless possibilities open to every corporation, just as there are to every individual."

He leaned forward in his chair and looked directly at me again. I felt like an awkward student in the presence of a master.

"In order for the company to stay healthy, and to grow, you always have to remember this: *The corporation is number one.* Put the interests of the corporation before your own interests, and before the interests of any owners, any employees, or anyone else.

"Never, never forget that. Take care of the corporation, first and foremost, and it will take care of you, and take care of all of its owners and employees and many others as well. But as soon as you place yourself — or anyone else, or the interests of any group — above the corporation, the business will suffer. And then everyone will suffer. *Everyone.*"

He settled back into his chair, but still talked with intensity.

"Some people I knew awhile ago — I knew them very well — had an experience we can all learn from. They had a family business, and it was very successful for many years. It had four different owners, all related. They made a lot of money from the business; it was a cash cow for many, many years. Then it ran into some problems. The problems were directly related to a lack of vision of the owners, because they became focused on the problems and lost sight of the opportunities.

"They ran into a recession, many of their methods and products became obsolete, and there were other problems as well. Again, there are opportunities there, even in recessions and in changes in society that make things obsolete. But they couldn't see the opportunities. They had gotten too complacent; they weren't changing with the times. And they were spending a lot of money on overhead, including a lot of employees who were pretty comfortable, and had been for years, and weren't working too hard. The business was still profitable, but far less profitable than it had been. So the owners had to take less out of the corporation.

"Two of the owners were willing to take far less money — but the other two had not managed their money well, and had gotten overextended, with big mortgages, big family support payments, all kinds of ongoing expenses. They'd gotten addicted to the income level they'd enjoyed for many years, and they couldn't cut back. Their CPA told them to cut back, or risk destroying the company — and they still couldn't cut back! They voted to continue drawing as much as ever out of the company.

"Do you see what they were doing? They put their own interests above the interests of the corporation — and they ended up killing the goose that was laying golden eggs for them, year after year.

The whole thing collapsed in a nasty family fight — it was sad to see. It was painful. They ended up liquidating, selling their assets for pennies on the dollar. They lost their company, and their steady stream of income, all because they neglected to put the company above their own interests.

"There's a lot to learn from this. One thing is this: Don't get overextended. When you have good years — and I hope you have many good years — use your profits to build up cash reserves, personally as well as in the business, so you have something to draw on during the lean years. But the most important thing is to *take care of the business first* — don't ever forget that."

"I won't." How could I? I had never seen Bernie so animated.

"Okay, I'm through preaching," he said, and he gestured broadly to the lawyer, as if he were handing him the stage. The lawyer handed me a large black three-ring binder, in a sheath, that contained all the articles of incorporation, by-laws, and stock certificates. Then he handed me the largest check I'd ever held in my hands.

SUMMARY

✳ In order to succeed, you must have a vision of growth and success. You've got to be able to clearly imagine how your company can quickly become profitable and steadily grow, increasing those profits, just as you've outlined in your five-year plan.

✳ For every adversity, there is an equal or greater benefit. That, in one sentence, is a key to visionary business.

✳ Spend some time in solitude, every day if you can. Review your goals, keep your dreams fresh in your mind. Focus on your plan. Always keep moving forward.

✳ Don't dwell on any pictures of failure; keep picturing success. No company should ever go into bankruptcy — it is a failure of the vision of the leaders of the company.

✳ There are no bad businesses, there are only poor managers. A good manager can take any kind of business and turn it around and make it successful. A poor manager can take any kind of business and run it into the ground.

✳ Your success may take a different route than you planned. The trick is to make a clear plan, a clear path to success, but then to be flexible enough to change your plans continually as new problems and obstacles and opportunities arise.

✳ The corporation is a brilliant invention, and has the capability to be used in infinitely creative ways. Your growth in business, as in life, is a never-ending process.

✳ Remember: The corporation is number one. Put the interests of the corporation before your own interests, and before the interests of anyone else, and it will take care of you, and take care of all its owners and employees and many others as well.

KEY FIVE

\||/

Plan your work and work your plan:
the employee handbook, benefits,
profit sharing, and stock options.

W E BANKED THE CHECK, and immediately
started spending it. I worried about
how quickly it was dwindling, but we
were spending according to plan. When we
received our first paychecks from our infant corporation, I was more concerned than elated; I worried that we might burn through our limited
resources too quickly, and that those regular paychecks might not continue.

I realized, though, that these worries were not
based on visionary thinking. I tried not to even
imagine the worst-case scenarios that would come
to mind; I tried to let them go as soon as I became
aware of them. I tried to follow Bernie's advice and
focus on the plan: the long-range view, a year down
the road, and the short-term steps we needed to

take to keep moving toward that long-range goal.

I attempted to save some money, but noticed how quickly my lifestyle changed to accommodate my new income level. It was a modest income, but certainly greater than my previous one. I needed a car, a television — soon I was quite accustomed to spending nearly all my paycheck.

I didn't forget Bernie's story about the people who lost their business, however, and I arranged to have a modest amount withdrawn from my checking account every month and invested in a mutual fund. When and if my income increased, I vowed to increase the amount I invested regularly.

We didn't hear from Bernie for over a month. Then one day he called and said, "Mind if I drop by?"

"C'mon over!" I said.

He was there in almost no time — he must have called from somewhere close by. He strolled around and chatted with everyone. He seemed pleased with what he saw. Then we went into my little office in the back. He saw the business plan on my desk. Perhaps he sensed that I hadn't opened it since the day we incorporated.

"Have you heard the phrase, *Plan your work and work your plan?*" he asked.

"No...."

"It's good advice. It's very important. You've used your plan to raise capital — that's good. But now be sure to keep working your plan. Don't just let it sit there and collect dust. Keep revising it, at least every quarter — ideally every month. Plug in your actual sales at the end of the month, and compare them with your projected sales. Same with expenses. Keep working your plan. Keep those goals fresh in your mind."

He stretched, as if he were comfortably at home, and then settled himself down into a chair.

"Good group of employees," he said. "Nice people. That's important. I always like to meet the owners, and ideally the employees, of any company I invest in — even if I'm just buying common stocks. I like to meet them surreptitiously, so they don't know who I am. That's why I just wandered into your company — that's the best way to see what's going on.

"Do you have an employee handbook of any kind?"

"What's that?" I asked, a bit sheepishly. I had no idea.

"Something you should handle as soon as possible. Ideally, as soon as you have any employees at all. There are two reasons for an employee handbook: one is for your protection, and the other is for the good of the employees, which is for the good of the business, of course.

"The part that protects you is some legalese I'll have my lawyer draw up for you — again, it's boilerplate stuff, it won't cost you much. It includes an agreement your employees sign when they're hired, and another agreement they sign when and if they leave the company — something they sign at the same time they get their severance check. Basically, the agreement says that they have received a copy of the employee handbook, and they understand that their employment is 'at-will', and that either your company or your employee is free to terminate their employment at any time, with or without cause. You also agree that any disputes will be resolved by arbitration, if necessary.

"This agreement protects you from lawsuits and helps you avoid legal conflict. Here's some valuable advice: *Avoid legal conflict; find ways to solve problems without lawyers.* Lawyers are paid to start fights — if it goes into the courts it becomes a war, and a war is by definition a lose-lose proposition. Nobody wins, except the lawyers. An aware business owner has no need for lawyers, just as every truly conscious person has no need for lawyers, except for peaceful purposes — advising on certain matters, or going over contracts."

I had an impulse to ask him exactly what he meant by "truly conscious," but he went on quickly, and for some reason I didn't feel comfortable interrupting.

"Learn to settle all conflicts without using lawyers, and you'll live a lot longer and prosper a lot more."

I wondered if Bernie was a fan of Spock in *Star*

Trek: Live long and prosper.

"The other part of the employee handbook — the fun part — spells out all the employee benefits. Do you have any benefits you've given your employees yet — in writing?"

"Not in writing," I said. "None of them have been with us for very long ... we've talked about paid vacations, and sick leave — we're calling them 'wellness days', so they don't have to pretend to be sick to take them. I don't think we can afford health care yet, but we all want to set up something as soon as possible."

"Good," said Bernie. "Let me give you my opinion about benefits — of course, it's your business, you run it the way you see fit, but I've found over the years that it's best for the company to offer the best benefit package possible. You aren't making much money yet — but you can start with a very generous number of vacation and sick-leave days. I mean *wellness* days — I like that phrase. Vacations don't really cost you much out of your pocket. And they generate a lot of goodwill. Give them their birthdays off, too, and a bonus for their birthday — even if at first it's so small it's almost just a token thing. They'll appreciate it, believe me.

"Give bonuses at Christmas, on their birthdays, and at the end of your fiscal year — even if at first they're small. Then visualize those bonuses growing larger and larger."

This struck me as an exciting idea.

"Get health insurance as soon as you can. Everybody needs health insurance these days — medical costs are ridiculous, astronomical. As soon as you're profitable, I'd get a dental plan, too — those are actually fairly reasonable in terms of cost, and they're great to have. Most people use their dental plan a lot more than their medical plan.

"Every company should be able to provide medical and dental coverage for their people, without it costing the employees anything. If they can't, something is seriously wrong with their business concept in the first place. It really irritates me when I hear business owners whining that they can't afford to pay medical benefits for their employees, whether the company's large or small. If they can't afford it, they're doing something wrong, because medical coverage doesn't cost that much — it's a minor part of an employee's salary."

I had on occasion had similar ideas about medical benefits. It felt wonderful to have someone as experienced as Bernie verify my feelings.

"And a pension plan is really important — have you looked into that?"

"Not really," I said. "We want to do something in the future, but we haven't given it much thought."

"There are some great pension plans that are based on your profits — if you don't make a profit, you don't fund the plan. So it doesn't hurt the company in the bad years. But you can contribute up to 15 percent of the total amount of salaries employees receive — including bonuses — into a tax-sheltered plan. It builds over the years, and they have something for retirement, something substantial. And they can even borrow against it, for housing, education, and medical emergencies. And the employees don't have to put any of their own money into it. I'd look into it right away, and present it to your employees, as soon as possible, even before you're profitable. That gets everyone motivated to cut costs and increase sales. It gets everyone thinking like an owner.

"The cash bonuses I mentioned are the other important thing. Let me tell you a story — do you have any coffee?"

"Oh, yeah Bernie, sorry!" I got up, embarrassed that I had been such an inconsiderate host. "Do you want anything else?"

"No, I'm fine — let's go out to lunch later, if that's okay with you. But I could go for a cup of coffee...."

A few minutes later, we settled down with a fresh cup of hot coffee, and Bernie told his story.

"Years ago, *eons* ago, when I was in the hotel business, I got a job offer in Switzerland, to manage a hotel. This was way before you were born, back in the last Ice Age. I went to Switzerland and toured the hotel — it was a mess, literally. The building was a mess. It was losing money. Employee morale was horrible. Service was horrible. There was a lot of what they call 'shrinkage' today: *shrinkage* — that cracks me up! It's a — what do you call it? — a euphemism for *theft*. Silverware, towels, toiletries, food, *paint* — you name it — kept disappearing at an alarming rate. The employees were paid on the bottom end of the pay scale, and had no kind of pension plan or profit sharing, almost no benefits at all. There was no management-employee rapport — there was a lot of resentment, in fact. Employee turnover was really high, which costs a company a lot more than most bean counters realize.

"I went to a meeting with all the owners, all the stockholders of this hotel. We sat around a big oval table — there must have been twenty or thirty people there. I told them I would accept the job, on one condition — they would have to agree to a formula I would implement, a simple formula: One-third of the profits would be plowed back into the hotel, one-third given to the employees as a cash bonus, and one-third would go to the shareholders.

"You should have seen their reaction! They looked like they thought I had lost my mind! They didn't seem to mind plowing money back into the hotel, but the idea of paying the employees as much of the profits as the owners were paid really got them worked up.

"I told them if they wanted me for the job, those were my terms. It was not negotiable.

Besides, I pointed out, they weren't making any money anyway! The place was losing money! Lots of money! Isn't it a lot better to get 33 percent of something than 100 percent of nothing?

"They ended up hiring me for the job — they must have been desperate. The first thing I did was to get all the employees together and tell them about the profit-sharing program. They would get one-third of the profits — as much as the owners were getting.

"You wouldn't believe the change in morale — well, I bet you would, come to think of it. The service improved *immediately*. And employee theft dropped to almost zero. The employees were thinking like owners, knowing they were going to benefit from the profits.

"After my first year there, the employees got a check out of the profits equivalent to about two weeks' pay. A few of the stockholders were still whining about the arrangement, but we had turned the business around and made it profitable. I left after seven years, and at the end of that time the employees' profit-sharing bonus was equivalent to over *eight months'* pay. In cash. Stockholders were happy. Employees were *ecstatic*. The guests were happy. The hotel looked great. It was a win-win-win-win situation."

He reached for his coffee with those long, delicate fingers.

"That's impressive, Bernie."

"Yeah, I did pretty well in the deal, too. They gave me stock in the company, and I got profits both as an employee and as a shareholder. I recommend that you set up something similar. The percentage may be different in terms of what you have to plow back into the company — though a third of the profits invested in expansion of the company is usually a good amount to invest. But, above and beyond what you plow back into the company, I recommend you split whatever's left over fifty-fifty between owners and employees. Of course, any owners that are also employees get paid out of the employees' pot as well as the owners' pot, because they're fulfilling two separate roles. Owners deserve to be well paid for their investment or their energy or vision or whatever it was that got them into that position. But employees deserve to be well paid, too, out of the profits of the company.

"Here's what I firmly believe, and my experience has borne it out — in fact, it's a self-fulfilling truth: *Give away half your profits to employees, and the company will do so well that, in the long run, you'll make much more as an owner than if you had kept all the profits.* It's win-win profit sharing.

"I think *all* businesses should have profit sharing, even the tiniest little mom-and-pop operations. Profit sharing that includes *everyone.* There's no excuse for not doing it — it's just good business. In the long run, owners will make more money if they share profits generously with everybody, even part-time workers. Everybody wins in the deal.

"Even the smallest company — say one with a single, part-time employee — could set up something. Just say to your people, 'Look, we're going to give you some of the profits. We don't know how much; we don't know if we'll be profitable or not. But if we are, you'll see a share of it.' "

I had been thinking that profit sharing was something we would do later, once we were profitable. Now Bernie was showing me how we could set it up even before we were profitable. I made a mental note to talk to everyone about it.

"I'd like to see *every* business set up profit sharing," Bernie said. "I'd like to see the *post office* set up profit sharing. Can you imagine? Run it like a private business and share the profits. McDonald's should set up profit sharing, and get their employees off that ridiculously low minimum wage, too. How can anyone live on minimum wages these days, and keep a roof over their heads? It's a mystery to me. I'd even pay more for a Big Mac if I knew they paid higher than minimum-wage salaries, and had profit sharing. I'd support that business, and so would a lot of other people.

"What if the *government* had profit sharing? Think of that! There's certainly some creative way to set it up — the government's just a business — a *huge* business, with way too many bureaucrats and agencies and special interests, but they're a business nonetheless. All their different offices could have different goals — especially cost-cutting goals. If the managers and employees cut, say, 20 percent of their costs, they get a 5 percent bonus. Something like that. There are all kinds of things that could be done, if they'd be motivated to think creatively — and that's what profit sharing does. Giving employees bonuses for money-saving ideas is another great way to share profits.

"Your employees are your greatest asset. You can have the greatest products and services in the world, but if you don't have good employees creating those products and doing those services and selling and marketing your products and services, and handling your accounting and keeping expenses down and managing cash flow, you've got no business — you've got a series of severe headaches.

"So give your employees great benefits as soon as you are able to — especially profit sharing. You know what profit sharing does, bottom line? It instills pride of ownership in employees. After all, what is ownership in a business — what does it mean? It primarily means you get a share in the profits when the business is successful. It can also mean you get some kind of say in how the business is managed — though not always. But as an owner, you're an idiot if you don't give employees a say in how the business is managed — they're in the trenches all day, doing their job, and they can see far more clearly than you can what the details and frustrations of that job are. They can often see how to improve their performance better than you can — not always, but often. They certainly have a perspective you don't have. So if you encourage them to think like managers, and pay them like owners, you give them pride of ownership. You give them job satisfaction. And they'll work hard for you, believe me. I've seen it happen over and over."

Bernie was animated, and it wasn't just because of the coffee. His spirit was inflamed with his ideas. I grabbed a notebook and started making notes.

"There's one final piece to your benefit package: an ESOP — an Employee Stock Option Plan. It's the last piece you'll want to put in place, later on, once the company is worth something.

"Through an ESOP, you can give — or sell — a significant piece of your company to your employees. The largest amount of stock goes to key employees, employees you would sorely miss, employees you want to keep working for you, but make sure *every* employee owns some shares of stock, even the part-time high school kids in shipping, if they stay with you long enough. Then they'll not only be acting like owners, they actually will be owners. A good accountant can help you set it up. But wait a few years, until your stock is worth a significant amount of money.

"Once you're profitable, you can actually start pretty quickly with a phantom stock program. Have you heard of that?"

"No...."

"Phantom stock is a brilliant invention. You issue shares to all your employees, in a simple, written agreement — only they're phantom shares. You can make up any kind of rules about phantom shares you want — that's the beauty of the system. Typically, you guarantee the employees you will pay them a bonus equal to the profits those shares represent: If a key employee's phantom shares are worth 4 or 5 percent of the company, for example, which is a common arrangement in a small company, they would be guaranteed 4 or 5 percent of the profits every year as long as they stay with the company — or if the company is sold. If they leave, however, the shares are worth nothing — so they have additional motivation to stay with the company. Eventually, over a period of years, your Employee Stock Option Plan replaces their phantom shares with *real* shares — and they become full-fledged owners.

"I know you've only got a few employees — but there'll be more."

"Yeah, we really need a receptionist, and someone in shipping..."

"There you go. Treat them like adults, treat them like valuable assets, and they'll act like adults, and they'll become valuable assets. Through cash bonuses and pension plan building and, eventually, owning stock in an ESOP, all of your employees that stay with you can, over time, amass wealth and build for an abundant future. Call it the Get Rich Slowly with Marc Program, or whatever you want to call it. You can probably come up with a better name than that." He seemed amused with himself.

"Your ideas are very generous," I said.

"Some people have accused me of being too generous — 'generous to a fault' — but I look at it this way: It is far better to be too generous than too stingy; it is better to give too much vacation time than not enough; it is better to give too many perks than not enough; it is better to be too laid back than too stressed out; better to be too relaxed than too driven; and far better to be too forgiving than too judgmental."

He smiled broadly and reached for his coffee. I reflected that, when someone is speaking the truth, everyone knows it's the truth because it is obvious. As the founders of our country said, truth is self-evident. Bernie went on:

"The business is a vehicle to realize your dreams. Work with all your employees so they can realize their dreams as well — whether their dreams lie through continued work with the business or eventually outside of it. Have them all do a five-year plan, unless they don't feel comfortable doing that — some people have difficulty projecting that far in advance. But work with them to help them imagine their future, in the same way I encourage you to work on your future. It's a win-win situation for you and your employees. Not only does it help them realize their dreams, but it engenders great employee loyalty. It makes them know they are a vital part of the team.

"Oh, one more thing, and then I'll let you go. This is something that should be obvious to every supervisor and employer, but it isn't: When you praise an employee — and you should praise them as much as possible — praise them publicly, in front of others. When you have to criticize them, or correct their work in any way, do it in private. This is a simple key to good management, one that should be taught to everyone, including every parent and everyone in a serious relationship."

I scribbled several pages of notes after Bernie left. I felt like heading it, "The Gospel According to Bernie."

SUMMARY

✳ *Plan your work and work your plan.* Keep revising your business plan, putting in actual sales figures and comparing them with what you had projected. Keep your goals fresh in your mind.

✳ Create an employee handbook that protects you as an employer from spurious lawsuits and spells out a generous package of benefits for each employee.

✳ Avoid legal conflict. Find ways to solve problems without lawyers. An aware business owner has no need for lawyers, except for peaceful purposes.

✳ Every company — large or small — should have generous paid vacations, medical and dental insurance, pension plans, and profit sharing.

✳ Give away half your profits to your employees, and the company will do so well that, in the long run, the owners will make much more than if they had kept all the profits. This is win-win profit sharing.

✳ Through a profit-sharing plan and a pension plan, and eventually through phantom stock and an ESOP — employee stock option plan — every employee that stays with the company can, over time, amass wealth and build for an abundant future.

✳ Praise an employee publicly. Correct their work in private.

✳ It is far better to be too generous than too stingy; it is better to give too many perks than not enough; better to be too relaxed than too driven; and far better to be too forgiving than too judgmental.

KEY SIX

\\\||/

Avoid management by crisis:
Make a clear annual goal.

I TOOK BERNIE OUT to lunch a few weeks later; it was the first time our little company picked up the tab. It wasn't a large tab; Bernie was happy to eat in a hamburger joint with formica-topped tables. He was happy to eat anywhere that served ham sandwiches on white bread.

I told him about our latest projects; he seemed very interested, not so much in the projects themselves, but in what they would cost and what we projected they would do in sales. We had come up with a "feasibility study" for each project: Our marketing director projected the first year of sales, and our financial department — our part-time book-keeper and I — projected expenses and profits. Bernie seemed impressed.

"You seem to be going after projects, making

63

them happen," he said. "That's important. Don't just sit back and wait for great things to fall in your lap. Decide what you want and go out there and get it. Do you have a clear goal of the sales you want to achieve for the year?"

The question caught me a little off guard; I hesitated for a moment. It was in the business plan, but it didn't come to mind right away.

"The number should be right on your tongue," Bernie said. "It should be *emblazoned* in your mind. Write it down and stick it in front of your face. Put it on your desk, put it in your billfold with your money. Write it on your bathroom mirror: your sales and your profits for the year.

"I read a very interesting thing in the paper a while ago. A company was struggling, and some of the managers of a certain division bought the division from the parent company and spun it off as an independent company. It was doing something like four million a year in sales, and was losing money. The new president of the company went to the employees with a plan to achieve something like 34.23 million in sales in five years. His plan precisely spelled out what they needed to do to reach that exact goal of 34.23 million in sales over a twelve-month period.

"And you know what? After five years they reached that goal — they nailed it right on the head, exactly 34.23 million dollars. That shows you the power of a detailed plan, and a clearly defined, specific goal.

"*Keep your mind focused on your goal.* Don't let doubts, fears, and 'small thinking' undermine that goal. Don't think too small — if you do, the company you create will always remain small. Your company reflects your mind; it reflects your dominant visualization."

I couldn't help smiling; hearing this old white-haired man use the word "visualization" again seemed somehow incongruous. I certainly agreed with what he was saying, however. And he obviously backed up his theories with a lot of experience. Bernie continued on, unconcerned about my responses to his words.

"If you can hold a vision of your company as successful, profitable — with specific numbers, always growing — your company will continue to grow and succeed. But if you keep focusing on the difficulties involved in growth, all the problems involved in the day-to-day operations of the company, personality disputes, problems with getting new products out and with suppliers and distributors and cash flow and so on and so on, you'll end up creating nothing but problems and getting nowhere.

"But if you keep focused on a vision of your success, if you keep a clear picture in your mind of where you want to be one year from now, and even five years from now — if you can do that — you'll end up aligning the exact forces you need to bring about your success. Keep focused on a clear goal, and the universe will work out the details."

That phrase had an impact — I wouldn't forget that phrase! Could it really be that simple — if you keep focused on a goal, the universe would work out the details? Bernie went on, speaking with absolute confidence, as if everything he said was the obvious truth.

"Only you can create your success, and only you can block your success. If your visualization of success is stronger than your doubts and fears, you'll succeed. It's that simple, in my experience. If you let your doubts and fears overwhelm you in any way — whether it's all the little doubts and fears about problems that come up on a daily basis, or major doubts and fears about achieving your goals in general — those doubts and fears will undermine your success. You'll end up creating that which you doubt and fear rather than the goals you desire.

"You've got to keep the big picture in mind, and keep assuring yourself that you can achieve the big picture. You've got to be your own coach, and your own cheerleader."

A waiter came by. "Okay, I'll have another cup of coffee," Bernie said. Then he continued, with enthusiasm. He sounded somewhat like a coach and a cheerleader.

"Richard Bach once said — I think it was in *Illusions* — 'argue for your limitations, and they are yours.' When you argue for your limitations, you always win the argument. If you keep thinking *it's so hard to succeed,* then it will be very difficult for you to succeed.

"Success follows a line of thinking that is focused on success. Failure follows a line of thinking dominated by doubts and fears. Your dominant thinking will always prove itself to be true. It cannot be otherwise. It is a law of nature. All thought becomes self-fulfilling."

He sipped on his coffee. I hoped I could remember his words.

"There are just two styles of management, as far as I'm concerned: management by crisis, and management by goals. The people who are caught in the management-by-crisis trap get so focused on the day-to-day problems that they never have time to step back and see the big picture. They're always working *in* the business, and never have time to work *on* the business. The day-to-day details become all-consuming, and their vision of the future is lost. They probably had some kind of vision in the first place, or at least some kind of dream, but all their anxieties around day-to-day problems have eroded the dream, and finally destroyed it. It has no power anymore.

"A dream is a fragile thing — yet it can be the most powerful thing in the world. But it needs to be constantly reinforced, so that it becomes firmly rooted in the subconscious. Doubts and fears need to be minimized. The dream needs to be supported by a concrete, achievable plan. Then the magic happens: All kinds of forces you never dreamed of come into play and help you manifest your dream. I definitely believe it's a form of magic — and I've seen it happen over and over in my life.

"God, I get to talking so much I forget to eat."

I felt a wave of affection for Bernie, as he picked up his ham sandwich with his long white fingers. The guy was more than a businessman — he was a magician. He understood visualization. He understood magic. And he used his power to create a great deal of good in the world.

Summary

✳ Have a clear goal of the sales and profits you want to achieve for the year *emblazoned* in your mind.

✳ Don't let doubts, fears, and 'small thinking' undermine your goal. Don't think too small — if you do, the company you create will always remain small. Your company reflects your mind; it reflects your dominant visualization.

✳ If you can hold a vision of your company as successful, profitable — with specific numbers, always growing — your company will continue to grow and succeed. But if you keep focusing on the difficulties involved in growth, you'll end up creating nothing but problems. If your visualization of success is stronger than your doubts and fears, you'll succeed.

✳ If you keep a clear picture in your mind of where you want to be one year from now, you'll end up aligning the exact forces you need to bring about your success. The universe will work out the details.

✳ There are just two styles of management: management by crisis, and management by goals. Those caught in the management-by-crisis trap are always working in the business, and never have time to work on the business. Their vision of the future is lost.

✳ A dream is a fragile thing, yet it can be the most powerful thing in the world. But it needs to be constantly reinforced, so that it becomes firmly rooted in the subconscious, and it needs to be supported by a concrete, achievable plan. Then the magic happens: All kinds of forces come into play and help you manifest your dream.

KEY SEVEN

\|||/

Give abundantly and reap the rewards.

W E WALKED BACK to the office taking a longer, more scenic route, skirting the edge of a park. We needed a bit of exercise after that lunch.

"This is a beautiful part of the world," Bernie said. "And it hasn't been destroyed by mindless industry."

It was surprising to hear such a pro-business person talk of "mindless industry," but then Bernie was always full of surprises.

"It's a crying shame the way business has polluted so much of the planet," he said. "And it's all their fault. They have no one else to blame. It's the managers of the corporations, who think that the most important thing in the world is the amount of money they make for shareholders — and for themselves, of course. And that's not the most important thing — it *is* important, but there are far more important things, such as the quality of life for all of us that share this beautiful, fragile planet of ours."

I couldn't help but smile as this old man in a brown suit with flashy gold cuff links and tie tack talked about our beautiful, fragile planet.

"Let me say this about business ownership. With ownership comes responsibility. Whatever you own — whether it's a house, a car, or a business — you're responsible for it. You're responsible for maintaining it, and you're responsible for its impact in the world.

"You have to maintain your house, or it loses its value. You have to maintain your car so it doesn't pollute too much — that's the law. And business owners have a responsibility to maintain their businesses, which most of them think means to make it grow and make it more and more profitable. And that's important. But there are other aspects of ownership a lot of owners just don't see — or don't care to think about — and their blindness, their lack of vision, creates a lot of problems in the world.

"The owners of a business also have a responsibility toward their employees, and toward the environment. Just as they want to create happy and healthy lives for themselves, owners are *responsible* for creating healthy and happy lives for their employees. This is where a lot of companies — large and small — blow it. Those large manufacturers who move their operations to another country so they can pay their employees dirt-poor wages and pollute the environment are asking for major trouble down the line. They put profits first and foremost and ignore everything else. Their workers suffer in poverty. They pollute the environment.

"What they have to come to realize is that they're responsible for the welfare of their employees, and the welfare of the environment. Ownership has responsibility to these things as well as to the bottom line. In the long run, supporting employees and helping the environment heal again is *good* for business, good for the bottom line. Henry Ford understood about paying employees well: He said he needed to pay them well, because he needed them to be able to buy his cars. That makes great sense. Pay your people well, and they'll have money to spend. It's good for the whole economy, which is good for your business, and every other business."

We walked in silence for a while. Then he shook his head sadly and went on.

"This kind of mindless, amoral ownership — or, in many cases, *im*moral ownership — that's so prevalent today is the main cause of pollution, and one of the major causes of poverty as well. Pollution and poverty mean a decline in the quality of life for *all* of us, because we're all in this boat together."

He stopped and gazed into the park. His eyes had that Yoda-like look of sadness and humor.

"So take care of your people and take care of your environment, even if your bottom line is a little less spectacular as a result, at least in the short run. It's money well spent. If you can't run a business without exploiting people or polluting the planet, you shouldn't be in that business in the first place. No one should. I don't care what any CEOs may claim: *Every* business, every industry, can minimize pollution. We're all responsible for cleaning up the mess we've made. And we should do it, without excuses, without procrastinating.

"Look at the auto business — a major contributor to worldwide pollution. Henry Ford knew he could build a car that burned a relatively clean alcohol fuel made from corn or soybeans, but his old friend Rockefeller talked him out of it, because Rockefeller was in the oil business. I'll bet you if they could have had the foresight to see the pollution that decision created, Rockefeller would have gotten into cleaner fuels, and this world would be a healthier place to live in. The auto companies have a major challenge ahead of them. They should quit procrastinating and create vehicles that burn clean fuels."

He was, once again, surprisingly animated for a man of his age. He looked for a moment like an old King Lear, raging at the storm.

"What can you and I do about it? We can certainly make our views known to the powers that be. And here's something you can do that will have a global impact: As soon as you start making a profit, give a generous percentage of that profit to organizations working to improve the world. Donate generously, both through your company and as an individual.

"*Every* corporation should donate generously. If every profitable business in the world gave even just 5 percent of their profits to non-profit corporations that are working to help people and the environment, think of the impact that would have!

"Shareholders would certainly continue to survive — and thrive — with 5 percent of their profits going to good causes rather than into their pockets. And that amount of money would have *incredible* impact! If half of the individuals on earth and half of the corporations donated even 5 percent of their income, we could end starvation around the world, house the homeless, send all our kids to high school and college for free, and clean up the whole planet.

"Start where you can, and do what you can. It'll all come back to you, believe me, in more ways than one."

These words came to mind, but I didn't feel comfortable expressing them: *Bernie, you're a visionary.*

We came up to Bernie's car — a brand new
Cadillac. I wondered if there was any contradiction
between all of Bernie's pro-environmental talk and
his choice of automobiles. I hoped there wasn't. I
felt Bernie deserved to ride in comfort and safety.
He opened his door, hesitated, and then said, "Do
you have time for a story?"

"Sure."

"Let's walk around the block again. It's good to
get some exercise."

"There's a nice little park over there, Bernie."

"Yeah," he said, "Let's take a stroll in the park."

We spent the next half hour or so in light conversation. Bernie admired the trees and the flowers, and could identify most of them. He stopped
at one point to smell the roses in somebody's front
yard. He told about the birds nesting in the eves of
his house. The young ones would occasionally fall
out of their nest, and Bernie and his wife would
guard them, and keep the cats away, until they
could get a ladder and return them to the nests. I
could just see Bernie climbing a ladder, probably
in his brown suit, risking his age-worn limbs to protect a fledgling bird. Then it occurred to me that
he was guarding our little fledgling company in the
same way.

He finally got to his story.

"I'll never forget one of my first jobs, right out
of high school," he said. "It was a small business, a
very successful one. I did grunt work; I did a bit of

everything. The owner made a lot of money — I mean, he was making a *fortune*. But he paid his people as little as possible, gave us no benefits at all, and tried to get the absolutely cheapest deal from every supplier he dealt with. He felt the more money he could squeeze out of his suppliers and his employees meant the more money he would put in his pocket. And he was right — *for a while*. He ended up making a great deal of money, for a while.

"But he didn't have the wisdom to understand that a person's quality of life is far more valuable than their bank balance — and the quality of his life was absolutely miserable. He had a constant battle with his employees: They were always leaving for greener pastures. He paid them no severance pay or anything, of course, so they'd just walk out the door when they got mad at him and leave the place in chaos.

"He was in a constant state of stress because some person had left, and he had to cover in an emergency situation. There was one crisis after another, continuously. He always had troubles with his suppliers, because he always pressured them to give him more for less money. He was never able to enjoy his money — he was too busy at work — and he died far too young of a heart attack while fighting a nasty lawsuit. So, in the long run, he ended up making far less money than he could have, because the stress killed him when he should have had many good years left.

"I despised him when I worked for him — everyone did — but I feel sorry for him now. He lacked understanding. He had no wisdom, no vision. Everyone I ever worked for taught me a great deal, but that man taught me more than anyone else. He taught me that the quality of our lives is much more important than the amount of money we make. The stress he created for himself was not worth all the riches in the world. He died alone, and miserable. His vast wealth was worthless to him.

"He didn't understand the law of giving and receiving. I'm convinced there's a special kind of hell — and it's right here on earth — for those who understand the principles of success well enough to amass wealth, but do not understand those principles well enough to be able to give to others.

"That was his fatal flaw — he couldn't give. I agree with Andrew Carnegie: I see no value whatsoever in amassing large quantities of money — the money simply becomes something that corrupts and weakens future generations. It is far better to give! Give your money away!

"I think it's *sick* that so many rich people are sitting on tens of millions, hundreds of millions — and *billions* — of dollars. Think of the good they could do with that money! Think of the number of homeless people they could house and feed . . . or of the positive environmental impact they could have!

"How much does one person need? That is the question. Ten million? Fifty million? Fine. Give the rest away — give it to your family, fine — ten million apiece will set them up for life. Then give it away! Circulate that wealth.

"Private businesspeople have done a lot of good for the world, but they could do so much more. Look at that guy who's guaranteeing college educations for a thousand inner-city kids, and who rebuilt their youth center! Did you hear about him?"

I nodded; I had just read about him in the paper.

"Look at the good he's doing with his money! If we could encourage more private citizens to act the way he's acting, we could solve the problems of the world.

"You should start with your own employees, and take care of them. Then find some worthy causes to support.

"That old boss of mine never supported anyone. Not even his own children. And certainly not his employees. He never understood that successful businesses, and successful relationships in general, are built upon *service to others*.

"We all have our own self-interest at heart — and that's as it should be. Each one of us has unique strengths, and a unique contribution to make to the world. Keeping our own self-interest in mind is absolutely necessary for us to fully realize our potential, our purpose in life.

"But people who have a little bit of wisdom understand that they can reach their goals only by serving others as best as they can, and helping others achieve *their* goals. It's a wonderful system: I scratch your back, you scratch mine. I can't scratch my own back very well; it's much more pleasurable to have someone else do it — and much more fun to give someone else the pleasure of having their back scratched.

"That old boss of mine probably didn't know he was a great teacher, in spite of himself. He taught me a great deal. He taught me how not to run a business, and that's important. He taught me the value of priorities. Money is not the final measure of a person's worth — there are far more important things: the quality of life we lead; the way we treat others, and treat our environment; the service we do for others; the amount of love and compassion we have for others; our purpose in life, and the degree to which we fulfill it; our positive contribution to others and to our planet. *That* is what is truly important in life. That is the measure of a person's worth.

"The most important words to remember and to try to practice, in business as well as in life in general, are *love, compassion, tolerance,* and *generosity* — for yourself and for others."

We walked back to his car in silence; his words were words to ponder.

SUMMARY

* As owner of your business, you have a responsibility to your employees, your community, and your environment.

* In the long run, supporting employees and helping the environment heal is good for business, good for the bottom line. If you can't run a business without exploiting people or polluting the planet, you shouldn't be in that business in the first place.

* Give a generous percentage of your profits to organizations working to improve the world. It will all come back to you, in more ways than one.

* The quality of our lives is far more important than the amount of money we make. And there is no value whatsoever in amassing large quantities of money. It is far better to give it away! Corporations and private businesspeople could do so much more to help people and heal the environment.

* Successful businesses, and successful relationships in general, are built upon service to others.

You can reach your goals only by serving others as best as you can, and helping others achieve their goals.

❋   Money is not the final measure of a person's worth — there are far more important things: the quality of life you lead; the way you treat others, and treat your environment; the service you do for others; the amount of love and compassion you have for others; your purpose in life, and the degree to which you fulfill it; your positive contribution to others and to your planet.

❋   The most important words to remember and to try to practice, in business as well as in life in general, are love, compassion, tolerance, and generosity — for yourself and for others.

KEY EIGHT

\\\\\\\//

"Love change, learn to dance, and leave J. Edgar Hoover behind."

S EVERAL MONTHS PASSED, quite quickly. I noticed the time seemed to fly by much faster now that I was working full-time for myself. The hours passed swiftly at the office. I'd often look at my watch and be surprised that it was so late. Sometimes I'd have a wave of panic, and think that there just weren't enough hours in the day — there just wasn't enough time to do everything that needed to be done. But then I'd think of Bernie, and how relaxed he seemed to be all the time, and how he always had time for a story or two. Somehow, that was reassuring to me; I just needed to do as much as I could each day, and leave the rest for tomorrow.

We didn't see or hear from Bernie for several months. Then one morning, our new receptionist buzzed me in my office on our new phone system.

"There's someone called Burtie or something who wants to talk to you."

"Burtie? Did he say Bernie?"

"He might have. I'm not sure."

It was Bernie, all right.

"New receptionist, huh?" he said.

"Well, she's been here a few months, but she's still learning...."

"It's really important for the receptionist to know what's going on. It's a very important job, you know, because that's the first contact everyone has with the company. I wouldn't expect her to know who I was — but be sure she knows your main people, and knows what's going on in general."

Bernie was being modest — the receptionist should have known about him, and we both knew it. I made a mental note to spend more time with her and fill her in on all the different people we regularly had contact with.

"Do you want to meet for lunch or something, later in the week?" he asked. "It's been six months already — do you have a six-month report for me?"

"Sure thing," I said, stretching the truth a bit. Well, I told myself, I'd have that six-month report by the time I saw him.

We met at his hotel room and sat out on the balcony overlooking the lobby, as usual. We'd come pretty close to our projections — we hadn't quite reached the sales we had hoped for, but were getting close. And some unexpected expenses had come up, like the need for a new phone system. I was certainly glad we had added an additional 15 percent for contingencies to our projected expenses, as Bernie had told us to. If we hadn't have done that, we would have been in trouble.

"This is a good report," Bernie said. "You're planning your work, and working your plan. Keep revising this baby — don't get complacent. Your ship has to have a course."

I told Bernie the business didn't feel like a ship to me — it felt more like a big old barge that was just sitting there at the dock, going nowhere. It felt like we were little tugboats, pushing and pushing the barge, and the barge wasn't moving at all.

"That's an interesting analogy," Bernie said. "It reflects your image — your visualization — of the business, and it shows you believe your business is *stuck*. You've got to change that visualization; you've got to get it moving. If you see the business as a barge, so be it — but start to imagine that barge is moving, slowly at first perhaps, but moving. Then watch it gain momentum, and move with its own power, so you won't need your little tugboats. Watch it cruise through the water, with you carried along on it, completely supported by it. Watch yourself enjoying a great ride!

"Believe me, as soon as you can change your mental concept of it — your visualization of it —

the business will change."

I told him I believed him.

"I heard a fascinating report on the radio the other day," Bernie said, as his ham sandwich arrived from room service. "It was about the CEO of Pepsico — I didn't catch his name, but I've heard it before and should probably know it. Anyway, in his five years with the company, profits have been up 30 percent per year, every year.

"He said his success is due to the fact that the company follows three simple rules, which are easy to remember. I thought they were very creative. His three rules are: (1) love change; (2) learn to dance; and (3) leave J. Edgar Hoover behind."

I gave him a somewhat quizzical look.

"They require some translation. The first rule is obvious: *Learn to accept change, even to love change.* The nature of life is change, and we either learn to love it, or resist the inevitable. Every company, like every person, is changing all the time. The world is changing all the time. Technologies change. People's tastes change. Their needs and desires change. Some companies have the vision to use that to their advantage; some don't. Those that don't, don't survive very long.

"A hundred years ago, selling buggy whips was a big, big business. But times change. Those that thought they were in the buggy whip business are out of business. Those that realized they were in the *travel accessory* business are still doing fine, selling leather upholstery or car phones or whatever.

"The second rule is *learn to dance*. That means dancing with all your customers, all your distributors, all your suppliers, everyone you work with. I like that terminology: The more we learn to dance with people, smoothly and skillfully, and give them what they want with the best possible service and quality of product, the easier it is to achieve our goals. Our working relationships with others should be a dance, not a struggle. Creatively working with people so that everyone's happy. Finding win-win solutions — dancing together! It's a wonderful way to put it.

"Do you remember the third rule?"

"Something about J. Edgar Hoover. . ." was all I remembered.

"*Leave J. Edgar Hoover behind.* Do you know what that means?"

"Not really — something to do with avoiding secrecy, or paranoia?"

"J. Edgar Hoover was famous — or infamous, rather — for his complete control of his employees' actions. His management style was completely dictatorial. Everything came from the top down; management told everyone exactly what to do. At least, that was the reputation he had.

"Leaving him behind means giving each employee responsibility to do their job in their own way. It's the kind of 'hands-off' management policy that J. Edgar Hoover would hate. Hire good people, clearly define their responsibility, and let them do it their own way. They're the ones in the trenches, doing their job all day. Get responsible people, and let them do their jobs as they see fit. As I've said before, treat employees like adults, and they'll act like adults. Treat them like children, and they'll act like children."

His words certainly made sense. He took a long, thoughtful sip of his coffee before he continued.

"Instead of management from the top down, it should be management from the bottom up. There has to be someone on top, one person responsible for the success of the whole operation, responsible for the vision, the long-range view of the company, and for the business plan, which translates the long-range view into the next short-term steps necessary to take. But the people doing the work should be completely responsible for managing their jobs. They should tell the president how they can best do their jobs, not the other way around.

"I've heard so many employers moan about how hard it is to find good people — I think that says more about those employers than it does about people in general. I've *never* had problems finding good people, never. Or keeping them. The world is full of good people, if they're treated with respect, treated as adults. If you assume they're responsible, they act responsibly. If you challenge them, they rise to the challenge. There are a few exceptions, of course, but the vast majority of people I've hired have done well in their work.

"There's just one simple rule I use in hiring people: Hire people who are *passionate* about that job. There are many different kinds of people in the world, just as their are many different kinds of jobs. Some jobs are repetitive, and require a lot of detail work and organization. There are a lot of people who genuinely like doing that kind of work — and other people who are driven nuts by that kind of work.

"One business leader I knew used to say there are three kinds of people — he was overgeneralizing, but he was making a good point. He said there were technicians, managers, and entrepreneurs. The technicians are the people that like to do the detail work. They enjoy the hands-on, nitty-gritty tasks. They like the sense of accomplishment a completed project gives them. All too often they do so well they are promoted to management positions, and a lot of them are ill-suited to management. They don't necessarily like to deal with people; they'd rather be doing the work itself.

"It takes a true manager to deal well with people. And it takes a true entrepreneur to take the risks necessary to start up new businesses, and new projects. Here's a good test: If you want to see whether a person is a manager or an entrepreneur, look at their garage — a manager's garage is neat as a pin, with outlines on the wall showing where to hang each tool, and an entrepreneur's garage is a mess, filled with half-completed or barely begun projects."

I had to laugh at that; according to that test, I was certainly an entrepreneur, not a manager.

"It's an overgeneralization, but it makes a good point: You've got to hire a technician for a technician's job, a manager for a manager's job. And don't hire entrepreneurs at all, because they won't be happy working for you, unless you have some real creative project they can develop, ideally something where they can eventually get equity ownership."

He stared at his ham sandwich.

"They must have a new chef. This sandwich is different than it was last week. Hmmm...."

He examined the sandwich carefully, analytically.

"This demonstrates another important business principle: *Be consistent.* In a changing world, people want as much consistency as possible. McDonald's is so popular because it is absolutely consistent, all over the country — probably all over the world, I don't know. I've never eaten at a McDonald's in Russia or China. But I know that anywhere you go in the U.S., it's absolutely the same hamburger. It's a lousy hamburger, but it's exactly what everyone has come to expect. Look at what a huge mistake Coca-Cola made when they tampered with their formula. They recovered well, with their 'Classic Coke', but they made a huge, expensive blunder because they forgot the principle of consistency.

"Try to be as consistent as possible with everyone you deal with. Try to create the best products and give the best service possible — and then be absolutely consistent in your execution. That's a challenge for you."

I had to agree.

SUMMARY

✳ *Love change.* The world is changing all the time. Those that have the vision to use change to their advantage survive and prosper.

✳ *Learn to dance.* Your working relationships should be a dance, not a struggle. The more you learn to dance with people, smoothly and skillfully, and give them what they want with the best possible service and quality of product, the easier it is to achieve your goals.

✳ *Leave J. Edgar Hoover behind.* Top-down, dictatorial management that tells everyone exactly what to do is inefficient, is prone to serious mistakes, and undermines employee morale. Hire competent people, clearly define their responsibilities, and let them do it their own way.

✳ Hire people who are passionate about their jobs, and who have the suitable personality for the job: Hire a technician for a technician's job, and a manger for a manager's job.

✳ In a changing world, people want as much consistency as possible. Try to be as consistent as possible with everyone you deal with. Try to create the best products and give the best service possible — and then be absolutely consistent in your execution.

KEY NINE

\\|||/

Reflect on the events that have shaped your life, and discover the core beliefs you have created for yourself because of those events.

THINGS WERE GOING fairly well for our business; we were certainly "planning the work and working the plan." At times there was even a new excitement in the air — the feeling of anticipated success. We had not achieved our goals, but we were making steady progress. The stodgy barge I had pictured the business to be was beginning to move a little bit, at least in my imagination.

A month or so passed, very quickly, before I heard from Bernie again. Then he called and invited me to his home for lunch. I jumped at the chance — I was curious to see what his home looked like. He lived outside of the city, in a beautiful, hilly area. I drove out there on a Friday afternoon. It was a lovely autumn day; the air was clear and delicious tasting.

As I drove out there, I told myself I had to get out of the office more often. I had to get away from the business, occasionally, both to get a fresh perspective on things, and to have some kind of a life away from my work.

The directions to Bernie's were a bit difficult; he lived quite a way off the main road. After roaming around a bit, I found his gate, which was open. He had a long driveway that went up a wooded hill and finally circled around in front of his home, a beautiful white structure nestled in the pines.

Bernie greeted me at the door wearing a sweat suit and moccasins. His hair was immaculately combed, as usual. He managed to look pretty sharp. We rambled through his home; he gave me a complete tour, often stopping to explain where a particular piece of art or furniture came from. Different rooms had different themes: The living room was filled with Native American art and his wife's original paintings, and had a look of the Southwest desert; his family room, off the dining room, was filled with Asian art: screens with exotic floral designs, paintings on cloth from Tibet and India. And, to my surprise, there was a room set aside for meditation and yoga, furnished sparingly, mainly with cushions, a sound system, and a sitting Buddha that radiated a quiet, peaceful energy.

Behind the house was a swimming pool with a hot tub on one end. The house and pool were on the top of a hill, and the view was inspiring. There was a large building off to the left, and another to the right, perfectly symmetrical. The one on the left was a guest house, beautifully furnished in an old Americana theme — it looked like a farm house from a century ago, complete with a hand pump on the edge of the kitchen sink. The building on the right was an artist's studio, with a large, airy central area and windows all around showing off the view.

Bernie's wife was inside the studio, a radiant woman named Lucia. The name fit her well: She was filled with light and laughter. She was working on a painting that shimmered color, reminiscent of South America, where she was from originally. Her thick hair was held back from her face with a colorful cloth — no, it was more than a cloth, it had sparkling jewels dangling from it.

She seemed very glad to meet me and shook my hand warmly. I felt happy for Bernie that he had found such a woman to be his wife — and happy for her that she had found such a man. There was a warm, obvious affection between the two.

Lucia kept painting and we went back into the kitchen, where Bernie had a lazy-susan on the table with two platters on it, one filled with meats and cheeses and avocado slices and other vegetables, and the other piled full of grapes and tangerines and exotic fruit like papayas and mangoes. He brewed up a delicious cup of coffee, as well.

After we feasted, we moved into the living room with the coffee and sat in front of a picture window that had a magnificent view of endless rolling pine-covered hills that became more and more luminescent in the distance. It was a view that inspired awe in the forces of creation.

We sat in silence in front of the window. Our lunch had been a late and leisurely one, and the sun was already getting low in the west.

"I sit here for hours, just staring out this window," said Bernie. "It's one of the ways I meditate."

Several minutes passed in silence. I saw exactly what Bernie meant by his statement. I felt extremely peaceful, happy just to be sitting there, comfortably in silence, watching the light play on the clouds and tree-covered hills.

Bernie finally broke the silence, speaking quietly. "It's important to meditate, in some form, whether it's sitting or walking or camping in nature or fishing, or whatever. Whatever you can do to be quiet for a while, and alone for a while, away from the radio and TV. There are all kinds of benefits of meditation: physical, mental, emotional, and spiritual.

"One of the greatest benefits of meditation is that it tunes you in to the still, small voice of your intuition. We all have many inner voices, and the way to identify the voice of our intuition is that it is calm and clear and self-assured — and it feels positive and supportive, always. Our intuition always knows what is perfectly right for us, in that moment.

"To be successful in business, you've got to be intuitive — you've got to learn to discover your intuition and to trust it. I don't know how to do that without meditating, in some form or other.

"I bet on you because my intuition tells me you're following your intuition. And that's all you need, ultimately, to be successful. Your intuition will guide you into doing the right thing at the right moment, and to doing what is in alignment with your purpose in life.

"You don't need an MBA, or accounting courses, or consultants. You don't need to copy other successful businesses. Just do what is in your heart to do — and you will be led, step by step, to reach your goals. The next step will always be clear to you — it will be obvious."

Several more minutes passed in silence. It was totally quiet in his living room, quiet as a temple. I don't think I've ever been in a place of total silence; it made me aware of my thoughts, which were going constantly, like a radio. It made me aware of how little meditation I had done. I felt honored to be able to sit in the peaceful stillness Bernie and Lucia had created in their home. He finally spoke again, quietly, in a way that somehow contributed to the sacredness of the atmosphere, rather than detracted from it.

"I've been thinking about something today,

something that affects the quality of our lives, and yet something that is rarely talked about. I've been thinking about the significant events that shape our lives, and how important it is to reflect upon those events, and discover the underlying beliefs we have created for ourselves because of those events."

I glanced from the window and looked at Bernie. He was sitting comfortably back in his chair, his hands forming a little temple in front of his chest, almost as if he were in prayer. Perhaps this moment was one of those significant events in my life.

"Every business reflects the consciousness of the owner. That's a fact. Yet it is so rare that business owners understand the importance of examining their lives — and examining how their minds operate — in order for them to create a better quality of life, and a more successful business as well.

"So many business owners sabotage themselves, needlessly, because of unexamined core beliefs about how the world operates. I had a mentor in business, many years ago. He was brilliant, and taught me a lot. Yet he also had some horribly negative core beliefs that affected his life and his business. He believed that you had to struggle to create a successful business — and so, of course, his business was an endless struggle. He believed you had to work hard, so hard that it adversely affected your health — and so, of course, he was in poor health, all through his later years. And he believed there wasn't enough time to accomplish what needed to be done, so he never took the time to enjoy life, to take vacations, to develop other interests. Those kinds of beliefs are self-fulfilling; *all of our core beliefs are self-fulfilling.*

"It's impossible to create a successful business without believing — deeply — that you are capable of building a successful business. It's impossible to live abundantly without believing that you deserve abundance, and that you can manage money wisely.

"My mentor was like a lot of successful business-people: He believed he knew how to create successful businesses, but he also believed a lot of garbage that really hurt the quality of his life. I wish I knew then what I know now — I would have told him what I'm telling you. Not that he would have listened, of course. His beliefs were too deeply ingrained; he wasn't open to change. He wouldn't even consider examining his beliefs to see how they affected his life. And the unexamined life is not worth living."

I had heard that before, but the way Bernie phrased it gave it new meaning.

"Thoreau said that. I don't think he meant it as a judgment call, to say that people who don't examine their lives lead worthless lives. I think he meant that, if you don't examine your life, the quality of the life you create is so far inferior to what you could create that it is probably better off not to have lived that life at all. We're here to grow, to constantly learn, to constantly build a better and better life for ourselves and others — and if we don't fulfill that promise, why live at all?"

There was another moment of silence.

"It's very important — in some cases *critically* important — to regularly take time to examine our lives. The first thing to do is to take a look at our past — as clearly and honestly as we can — and discover the important events and influences that have shaped our lives.

"We've all had these shaping events: the major events in our lives that have shaped the way we think, the way we perceive the world. The events and people that have given rise to our core beliefs about the world, about ourselves, about the nature of reality.

"All of us have had a wide variety of shaping events. Some have had a great many painful events like abuse or violence of other sorts. Some shaping events are the results of painful experiences, some are the results of powerfully positive experiences, some are the results of the simplest moment, the simplest word from someone at the right moment that we have carried with us ever since.

"Some of these shaping events have led to very good core beliefs — and those moments should be remembered, and those beliefs should be encouraged and supported. All of us have had someone in our lives who saw our potential and supported us in some way. Even kids in the worst circumstances usually have someone who inspires them in some way — a teacher or a parent or *someone*. Or else they find a wellspring of inspiration somewhere in themselves.

"We've all had glimpses of our genius, as children, and we've all had other forces that have sought to crush our genius, through doubt, through cynicism, through lack of faith.

"We need to reflect on these things occasionally. Those shaping moments that have had a negative impact on us need to be looked at, and we need to discover the negative core beliefs we formed as a result. Once those beliefs are identified, they can be let go of. Because they aren't true — they're simply self-fulfilling things that become true if we believe them. This is the process of becoming conscious — becoming aware of the forces that drive us, and learning how to act on those forces, how to shape our destiny, how to become powerful. How to achieve what we want in life.

"That's why it's so valuable to write an autobiography — I think everyone should write their autobiography. Or at least reflect on the moments that forged our core beliefs, at least describe and remember the shaping moments in our lives.

"Every one of us is a creative genius, in some way. And every child knows it! But as we grow into adulthood, we gather a collection of garbage beliefs that trash our belief in ourselves. It's important to examine those beliefs, and dump that garbage.

"You are capable of *anything* — anything your heart desires. There are no limits to what you can accomplish — *if you believe it to be true.* What you believe to be true becomes true, in your experience. So examine your beliefs, and create only those beliefs that empower you."

Bernie spoke with authority and eloquence; it was more like oratory than regular speech. His words were inspiring. I hoped I could remember them.

"When you believe in yourself enough, your most important desires will become *intentions* — and your intentions will manifest in reality. It's a law of nature. Intentions produce results.

"Our thoughts and our words are powerful — powerful enough to create what we want in life."

There was silence once again. The sky was a fragile eggshell blue painted with chimerical wisps of delicate pink clouds. The sun was beginning to set, in an awe-inspiring display of what is possible.

"So be it. So it is," he whispered.

SUMMARY

❋   It's important to get away from your business occasionally to gain a fresh perspective on your work and your life.

❋   It's important to meditate in some form, whether it's sitting or walking or camping in nature or whatever. There are all kinds of benefits of meditation: physical, mental, emotional, and spiritual.

❋   Through meditation, you can discover the calm and clear and self-assured voice of your intuition. To be successful in business, you've got to be intuitive — you've got to learn to discover your intuition and to trust it.

❋   Every business reflects the consciousness of the owner. Yet so few business owners understand the importance of examining their lives, and examining how their minds operate, in order for them to create a better quality of life, and a more successful business as well.

✳   We all have core beliefs created during child-
hood and young adulthood, and these core
beliefs are self-fulfilling. Our positive core
beliefs — such as the belief that we are capable
and creative — should be supported and
encouraged. Our negative core beliefs — such
as the belief that it is hard to succeed and can
only be done at great personal sacrifice —
should be identified and let go of. Our negative core beliefs are not true — they are simply
self-fulfilling; they become true if we believe
them.

✳   Every one of us is a creative genius, in some
way. There are no limits to what you can
accomplish — *if you believe it to be true*. When
you believe in yourself enough, your most
important desires become *intentions* — and
your intentions will manifest in reality. It is a
law of nature: Intentions produce results.

KEY TEN

\|||/

Evolve through the
three stages of a business:
infancy, adolescence, adulthood.

WAS GROWING TO ENJOY my time with Bernie immensely. I took notes after each of our encounters; my pile of notes was growing into a little book. I'd often page through the notes, and I'd always find something inspiring or useful — usually both.

Bernie called a few weeks after I had been to his house, and asked me to meet him in a state park area that was not too far from the city. I was only too happy to get out of the office — it had been a difficult week. I needed a break. And I looked forward to seeing Bernie again.

We met in the parking lot. Bernie was there when I arrived, dressed in his sweat suit, with well-worn running shoes, sitting comfortably on the hood of his car with his feet on the bumper. He looked like a large gargoyle hood ornament.

We walked through the woods, quite briskly at times, enough to work up a sweat. The trees were bursting with the brilliance of autumn.

He asked how the business was going. I told him we were close to our projections — but hadn't hit them. I was disappointed, I had to admit — I had thought the projections were conservative and we would not only be able to reach them, but substantially surpass them.

"What are you planning on doing in sales for the year?" Bernie asked.

This time I had the answer for him, immediately. It had become emblazoned in my mind; it was my most important goal. Bernie chuckled appreciatively.

"Don't worry if you're a bit short of your goals at first," he said. "It almost always happens that way. The growth of a business is an organic thing; it takes time. It has taken Nature many years to grow these strong, solid trees — it will take years for you to grow a strong, solid business."

He wandered off the path and over to a magnificent pine that towered over us. "Look at this tree," he said. He raised both hands and placed them high on the trunk of the tree, communing silently with it for a moment. "Our lives are like this tree — and your business is like this tree: It will grow and grow, until it casts its seeds to the wind . . . and many of those seeds will grow, and many of them won't.

"Some years, the trees get a lot of rain, and there's an explosion of growth. Some years, when it's dry, they barely grow at all. Sometimes there are years of drought, and they retrench, and don't grow at all.

"It's the same with your business...." The sentence wandered off a bit, and Bernie went wandering off as well, into the trees.

"Every business goes through three stages," he said, after we had trekked along for a while. "Infancy, adolescence, and adulthood. You're still in your infancy, so you have to be patient, just like you have to be patient with a baby. A business in its infancy has to be constantly fed and nurtured, watched and guarded. It's still vulnerable, and it has a big appetite. You have to keep giving to it, and you can't expect anything in return.

"But, as long as you're patient and you stick to your plan and keep your goals clearly in mind, one day you'll find your baby has become an adolescent. At this stage, it can support itself, but no one else. It's important at this stage that you don't try to treat it like a mature business. It's still young. Don't draw too much out of the business. Be very careful about expanding too quickly. Growth should be slow and steady, like these trees, or like a young man or woman.

"Finally, if you keep your visualization strong, your business will reach its goals, and become a true adult. It'll be mature, powerful, able to support you and many others abundantly.

"When you reach that point, I want you to do a few things: First of all, take a vacation. A long, well-deserved vacation. Then take regular vacations after that. You've got to get away from the business, every once in a while, to relax, and to gain a clearer perspective on your business and your life.

"When your business has reached adulthood, it can pay everyone a good salary as well as a substantial share of the profits. Keep salaries reasonable — competitive with industry standards, but on the generous side — and reward yourself and everyone else with abundant profit sharing.

"When your business has reached this point, here's something else I recommend: Send your parents a big bonus check, if your parents are still alive. Send it to them whether they need it or not.

"It's something I did, as soon as my first business started making money. I just did it on a whim, because I kept fantasizing doing it. But after I did it, I discovered it was one of the single best things I ever did. It totally surprised and delighted my parents, of course. But it was an even better experience for me. By making that gesture, I told myself, as well as my parents, that I was an adult now, and could support myself — and even support them if need be. It sent a powerful message to my subconscious mind that I was ready, willing, and able to create a mature, powerful company, one that could support me and others in abundance. It's far more than just a gift; it's a confirmation of your expanding power."

We reached a pond, nestled in the trees. Bernie picked up a stone and skipped it expertly across the water. It carved a long arc across the still surface, skipping ten or twelve times before it finally sank.

"Nice job, Bernie."

"I've had lots of practice."

I picked up a flat, round stone and gave it my best shot. It skipped once then sank abruptly.

"Hmmm, I guess I need more practice," I said. It had been more years than I cared to remember since I had skipped stones into a pond.

We spent the next twenty minutes or so playing like children. I finally found the perfect stone that skipped in a long arc, like Bernie's first one had done. I was surprised how good it felt, even though my arm ached. I was as elated as a six-year-old.

We strolled on, and Bernie picked up right where he had left off.

"Once your business is in its adulthood, use your money wisely. Always keep some in reserve, so the business has more strength to weather difficult times — and there probably will be difficult times; there are for nearly all businesses. The economy is cyclical. Those businesses that have cash reserves can weather all the cycles.

"You should have some personal cash reserves, too, that you can draw on and even loan back to the company if necessary. Don't get too overextended too quickly with big mortgage payments, a big vacation home, and other things that have a constant monthly payment attached to them. Live frugally for a while, pay off your credit card debt, and get ahead of the game with some substantial savings. Then you can go out and buy that vacation home, or boat, or whatever it is you desire.

"Once the company starts making profits, give away at least 10 percent of your profits: Give at least 5 percent of your profits to worthy organizations — there are hundreds of them that are worth supporting — and give at least another 5 percent to employees and friends and relatives and other worthy people and causes."

I was a little unclear on his concept. "How does this fit in with what you said earlier, when you said to retain what the business needed, and then split the rest between the owners and employees?"

Bernie explained carefully: "First you have your total pre-tax profit — the bottom line of the company's annual profit and loss statement, right?"

"Right."

"Then you need to retain in the company as much as you and your banker and your directors — or financial advisors, whoever you consult — feel the company needs. This is the amount you pay taxes on. So first you subtract your retained earnings and your taxes. Then take 10 percent of the remaining amount and give it away — half to worthy organizations and half to worthy individuals, including employees, and to local good works and so on. Then split the remainder between the owners and employees. At least, that's what I recommend. You may find a different formula that works better for you.

"Tithing 10 percent is not only generous, it's good business. It's great public relations for the company. But it's far more than that as well: In order to be really successful with money, you've got to give it away. There's something mystical about the tithing principle — it expands you, so that more money comes to you.

"Personally, give at least 10 percent away, too, so you're contributing on both fronts: business and personal. Don't use the excuse, 'I gave at the office.' Give at home and at the office. And a magical thing will happen: You'll never want for money. You'll be surrounded by infinite abundance. The universe will keep showering you with riches.

"Give to charities, give to friends, relatives, people on the street; give to environmental groups and human rights groups and children's organizations; give to your church if you go to church; give to the local soup kitchen, the local shelter, the abused women's center, homes for children, libraries, youth programs; give to anything and anyone that moves you to give. Just make sure it's at least 10 percent of your income. You'll never regret it.

"Once your business is successful, one of the greatest, most satisfying things you can do is to support all kinds of worthwhile things, and people, both through donations and investments. I donate to a lot of good causes. I'm doing my bit for the earth and for humanity: Greenpeace, Children International, Amnesty International, Sierra Club, World Wildlife Fund, the Nature Conservancy, the local homeless shelter, the list goes on and on. And I invest in all kinds of things as well, and I love it. It's just as gratifying for me as it is for the people I invest in.

"I'm investing in you, for example, helping in my way to make your dream a reality. And I'm enjoying it as much or maybe even more than you are.

"The more you give, the more you receive — and not just financially, though it's true financially. But you receive even more important things as well — satisfaction, contentment, fulfillment, joy. And even love.

"And that's the most important thing of all."

SUMMARY

* The growth of a business is an organic thing, just like the growth of a large, strong tree — both take time to develop. Both have years when growth is explosive; both have years when there is little or no growth. Be as patient with your business as you would be with a pine or oak seedling.

* Every business goes through three stages: infancy, adolescence, and adulthood. A business in its infancy has to be constantly fed and nurtured, watched, and guarded. You have to keep giving to it, and you can't expect anything in return.

* Once a business has reached adolescence, it can support itself, but no one else. It's important at this stage that you don't try to treat it like mature business. It's still young. Don't draw too much out of the business. Be very careful about expanding too quickly. Growth should be slow and steady.

✳   If you keep your visualization strong, your business will reach its goals, and become a true adult. It will be mature, powerful, able to support you and many others abundantly.

✳   Once your business is in its adulthood, use your money wisely. Always keep some in reserve, so the business has more strength to weather difficult times — and there probably will be difficult times; there are for nearly all businesses. The economy is cyclical. Those businesses that have cash reserves can weather all the cycles.

✳   You should have personal cash reserves, as well, that you can draw on and even loan back to the company if necessary. Don't get too overextended with big monthly payments; pay off your credit card debt and get ahead of the game with some substantial savings.

✳   Once the company starts making profits, give away at least 10 percent of your profits: Give at least 5 percent of your profits to worthy nonprofit organizations, and give at least another 5 percent to employees and friends and relatives and other worthy people and causes.

✳   The more you give, the more you receive — and not just financially. You receive even more important things as well: satisfaction, contentment, fulfillment, joy, and love.

KEY ELEVEN

\||||/

*Consider the mystical and spiritual
side of business: Practice your own
form of effective magic.*

WAS STILL STRUGGLING with a business in its infant
stage, and I was an exasperated and impatient
parent. When I look back on it, there were
deeper reasons for my frustration than purely
financial ones. On a deep level — on what Bernie
would describe as a core belief level — I had my
doubts and fears about everything I was doing. I
even doubted the validity of building a business in
the first place. I had deep core beliefs that if I succeeded in building a successful business, I would
lose my soul in some way: I would become con-
sumed by materialism, and forget my higher purpose in life.

I had insistent doubts and fears about the
direction my life would take if I were to build a successful business. Perhaps Bernie was aware of my

thoughts; perhaps he had gone through a similar stage when he was young. I wanted to ask him, but felt uncomfortable doing so. In light of all this, our next meeting was truly remarkable.

Several weeks passed before I heard from Bernie again. Then he called, on a Friday afternoon, and said, "Look, there's a full moon on Monday. Why don't you come out to my place in time for the sunset and moon rise? It's quite spectacular."

Bernie hadn't exaggerated. We watched the sunset from his living room and then went out by his pool to watch an almost unbelievably large, brilliant orange harvest moon rise slowly over the shadowy trees. The lights were on in Lucia's studio; she was apparently painting.

"On nights like this, I love to sit in the hot tub," Bernie said. "Care to join me?"

It seemed like a good idea. The night was cool; the tub was very warm. We had to get in slowly to avoid being burned. Bernie's body was lean and supple. It was quite a surprise to see him in such good shape.

"My favorite nights are the ones I spend alone in this hot tub," he said. "And in my study, and just strolling around the grounds, while Lucia is painting."

He exhaled deeply in the hot tub, several times, and faced directly into the rising moon. He looked much younger than his years. His eyes were large and clear.

"This kind of night, this full moon, makes me get metaphysical," he said. He chuckled softly, then spoke quietly but intensely.

"I've given you everything you need to understand the mechanics of successful business. If you can remember half of what I've said, and apply it, you'll achieve your goals. But I want to say something about the essence of business, the essence of life.

"We live in an exciting time. It used to be that science and metaphysics were considered to be almost polar opposites. They seemed to have two completely different methods: metaphysics was intuitive; science was rational. They were even violently opposed to each other at various times in our history. But, in the twentieth century, science and metaphysics merged. Physicists discovered what the metaphysical types had been teaching for centuries: It is only our crude sense of sight that makes it appear as if we are quite different individuals; we are in reality all one, in one vast ocean of atoms, eternally interconnected. And those atoms are composed of empty space, yet filled with whirling forces of energy and information. Buddhists have been chanting for thousands of years: 'Form is emptiness; emptiness is form.' Physicists have discovered this is true.

"Some people call it New Age!" He laughed at

the term. "There's nothing *new* in the new age. James Allen wrote *As You Think* in 1904! It's all in that book. Everything. Israel Regardie wrote *The Art of True Healing* in the 1930s. It's filled with powerful creative meditations; it's Western magic in a nutshell. The so-called New Age philosophy is the Perennial Philosophy that Aldous Huxley described — it's as old as humankind. . . .

"For myself, I've boiled its essence down to something that's very simple. That's the way it has to be, for me — it has to be simple and clear to have an effect in my life."

He sat in silence for a moment, gazing at the moon, before he continued.

"There are many paths up the mountain. And people must find what they need to find in their own way, on their own terms, and in their own words in the Perennial Philosophy — or the New Age or the spiritual quest or personal growth or higher consciousness or the Twelve Step programs or whatever else you want to call it.

"My parents were Jewish. But I didn't see, didn't really understand, the wisdom in my own tradition. I looked to the teachings of India as a young man, and I found answers and guidance.

"I learned about *dharma* — which means the teachings, the laws of the universe, and the importance for each of us to discover our higher purpose in life, our mission, and to realize that purpose and mission.

"I learned about *karma* — all of us are rewarded with the fruits of our thoughts and actions, whether those thoughts and actions are good or bad. The good person encounters goodness and success; the misguided person who doesn't understand *karma* encounters pain and failure. Each of us creates our own experience of the world; we have no one else to blame for our failures.

"I went to India as a young man...." He smiled at the memory. "I met a teacher who told me my mind was far too active. He tied a string to my wrist and tied the other end to a turtle, and told me to stay with that turtle for three days. And I did it. I have never been the same since." He laughed heartily.

"I learned about meditation in India: the importance of learning to sit quietly. I saw how, once our mind begins to quiet in meditation, our intuitive mind starts speaking to us, in a still, small voice. Actually, it has been speaking to us all the time, but we just never bothered to sit still for a while, and shut up and *listen within.*

"I learned to do yoga. That's why I'm in such good shape. That and my fruit juice regimen — I drink lots of fruit juice, morning and evening. And I do a bit of yoga every day, even if it's just a Salute to the Sun or two. My yoga teacher told me to close my eyes when doing yoga, and 'see God'. She said it so simply, so plainly, and I've never forgotten it....

"Then I came back to my country and looked

to the Christian tradition, and found answers and guidance. I realized that Christ had taught about karma when he said, 'As you sow, so shall you reap.' And St. Paul had taught about moderation — 'the Golden Mean' — just as Buddha had taught about taking the middle road, the path between all extremes, the path of moderation in everything.

"I read the Bible. The words of Christ are still brilliant today. It's sad to me that so many people proclaiming to be Christian somehow manage to ignore so many of the words of Christ. Like the right-wing types who want to carry firearms and build atom bombs and enforce the death penalty. What would Christ's reaction be to those people?

"And so many institutions have risen, churches and governments, proclaiming to be Christian, that have forgotten the words of their founder!"

He quoted easily, from memory: *"Love your enemies, bless them that curse you, do good to them that hate you, and pray for those who despitefully use you, and persecute you.... If you live by the sword, you die by the sword.... Turn the other cheek.... Judge not, lest you be judged.... He that is without sin among you, let him cast the first stone.... The Kingdom of Heaven is within.... Ask and you shall receive, seek and you will find, knock and the door will be opened unto you....*

"I looked at the traditions of indigenous peoples all over the world as well, and found answers and guidance. They all believe in the sacredness of the earth. Our earth is our Mother, and we must respect and cherish her. They all believe in worlds beyond this world of ours. They believe the dead have power, and need to be respected. We need to live in a way that our ancestors would be proud of, because the spirits of our ancestors are still with us. Just as Christians believe you can feel the spirit of Christ living in your heart, so indigenous peoples know they can feel the spirits of their ancestors, living and breathing through them.

"I have studied Western mysticism, too, and found answers and inspiration. I learned that real magic exists; I learned how to do magical rituals for health, problem solving, prosperity, love.... As long as you understand karma, magic is a powerful tool that can work for you.

"And that led me right back to Judaism, because much of Western magic is based on Judaism. And I finally found answers and inspiration within my own roots, right back where I started.

"The best way to express what is for me the simplest and most important truth — and this may or may not surprise you — is from the Twelve Step programs, begun by Alcoholics Anonymous. God bless Alcoholics Anonymous! The twelve steps are brilliant.

"The third step says, *I made a decision to turn my will and my life over to the care of God, as I understand God.* That leads right to the eleventh step, *I sought through prayer and meditation to improve my conscious contact with God as I understand God, praying only for knowledge of God's will and the power to carry it out.*

"That's it, in a nutshell — at least for me: *Just keep turning it over to God, asking to do God's will.* That's the one simple solution. Whenever you have a problem, turn it over to God — whatever you believe God or a Higher Power or the creative force of the universe to be."

There was a quiet pause, as Bernie gazed at the moon in silence. The silence, like the hot tub, was warm and satisfying. I felt no need to say anything. Bernie finally broke the silence.

"So, the most important thing for each of us is to reflect on what we believe God to be. What is God in our lives? What do we really believe? What makes sense for us? What is reasonable, for each of us, given our unique background and culture and beliefs? It's very important to reflect on this, and come up with something — because that conception of God can provide us with all the answers and guidance and inspiration we need to create the kind of life experience we dream of creating....

"Everyone has some conception of God, or a higher power, even if they think they're athiests. As I've said to many people many times before, if you don't believe in a higher power, go make a blade of grass. Or a cricket. Or a galaxy. Some power created those things — how do you describe that power? Chemistry? Then that's your higher power. Atomic energy? Then that's your description of what I choose to call God, the forces of *good*, of creation, of life.

"Here's my simple conception of God. It was within the Native American culture and teachings I found the words that work for me: God is the *Great Mystery*. We'll never understand God; God is the force of creation, eternally mysterious. God is the force within the atoms, the intelligence that forms the structure of all matter. God is the force within the galaxies, the force that causes stars to be born and to spawn life and to spectacularly die. God is the force that causes the simple elements that have been blasted out from those dying stars to combine and to form all living things, including molecules as complex as the DNA in every cell of our body. We'll never really understand those forces, in their essence. It's the Great Mystery of our existence.

"Do you believe in God?" He didn't give me time to answer the question.

"To me, this question is exactly the same as, Do you believe in the creative power of the Universe? Or, Do you believe a tiny seed can grow to a huge tree? Or, Do you believe in physics?

"The answer to all these questions is obvious to me — and has nothing to do with belief.

"Whenever you have a problem — business or personal — turn it over to the forces of creation, to God as you understand God. Most people call this process prayer, but you can call it anything you like. Just say, 'Well God (or whatever you want to call it, or him, or her), I put the problem in your hands — I'm turning it over to you. Just show me what your will is. Let me do your will.'

"Turn everything over to God; let God work out the details.

"Just keep asking to do God's will, and your problems will dissolve. You will be shown, step by step, intuitively, what to do.

"You never need to worry about your business once you really turn it over to God. For you aren't in charge of your business any more — God is the new president. And the chairman of the board as well.

"Just keep asking what God's will is, and you'll be guided in your business to do exactly the right thing for you. You might take the business in completely unexpected directions! It doesn't matter — God is showing you where and how to go. God is directing the show."

I had been completely absorbed in his words, trying to remember as many as possible. Then I suddenly became aware that I was extremely hot; my hair was soaked with sweat. Bernie read my mind.

"Let's get out of here," he said. "Enough is enough."

He plunged into the pool, and I followed. It was cold; it was exhilarating.

We toweled off and dressed again and went

inside the house, where Bernie opened the door of his refrigerator, revealing an entire shelf that was filled with a dozen different kinds of fruit juices. Each of us got a tall glass, added some ice, and made our own blend of juice.

Bernie's favorite drink was a mixture of cranberry juice and grapefruit juice: "A *virgin sea breeze*," he said. "That's what they call it in a bar. Sounds nice, doesn't it? Very poetic. In the morning, I add fresh squeezed orange juice to it. Sometimes I add ice tea."

It was cool and delicious, the perfect thing to have after that intense hot tub. We sat in his living room, in front of the picture window, and gazed at the hills bathed in the spot light of a brilliant full moon, which was now silvery white rather than orange.

We sat quietly, sipping our drinks, watching the silent moon. There was very little light in the room; the moon was the star of the show. I felt relaxed, in no hurry to do anything or go anywhere. I was just content to sit in silence. I reflected on how unusual that was for me — usually I was rushing along, always looking ahead, wanting something in the future, whether it was to finish a project or to get to some destination or to get a cup of coffee or a meal. I so rarely sat still and just enjoyed being in the present moment, with absolutely no desire for anything else to make me happy or fulfilled.

Bernie sat motionless. I did too, and I seemed to lose track of time. It seemed as if we sat there for just a few minutes, though the moon climbed quite high in the sky. It was getting late.

Bernie finally moved a bit, took a sip of his juice, and looked at me.

"I want to show you something before you go," he said. His voice was deep and quiet. "Here's a course in magic — a course in creation.

"All creation is magical, and we create all the time. So all of us are already magical beings. All of us are magicians. But a lot of us don't know it, that's all.

"Here's an entire course in magic — it's a short course, but it's all that's necessary. Let's see ... I need some paper...."

He got up and wandered off into the darkness. As he returned he adjusted the light in the room, turning it up a little. I noticed his lamps had adjustments, so he could carefully control the amount of light each one gave off. He handed me a pen, a sheet of paper, and kept another for himself.

"Draw one of these," he said. And he drew a large star in the center of the sheet, which covered over half the sheet of paper.

"This star is central to this teaching. I use a five-pointed star — you can pick a six-pointed star if you wish, or any number of points, or simply a radiant circle. The most important thing is to imagine that it is a star, and it's filled with light — shining clearly in front of you. In your meditation, focus on this light-filled star, and then let the light take whatever form it will. It may remain as a star, or it may change for you. It may be a person filled with light, with arms outstretched. In Western magic, the five-pointed star stands for Man, with arms outstretched. Man — or Woman — in the form of light, in the form of God, whatever you want to call it.

"Now, at the top point of this star, put these words:

God's will

"Or something similar, however you choose to define God. Choose whatever words work for you, whatever keeps reminding you to turn your desires, your goals, your problems — *everything* — over to God, or the forces of creation.

"Then, at every other point on the star, list something you want to create in your life, something you are passionate about. With a five-pointed star, therefore, you choose your top four goals, desires, dreams, and put one at each point.

"Putting it in this visual way is effective for many reasons. It forces you, for one thing, to keep asking yourself if what you are wishing for is God's will. This is important. It forces you, too, to just choose four possibilities, from the realm of all possibilities. So you have to prioritize: What are your four most important goals?

"Once you have chosen your goals and written them down, ask yourself: Am I truly ready and willing to receive what I'm asking for? Because you're going to receive it, and you have to be ready for it.

"Remember what Deepak Chopra says, *'Within every desire is the seed and mechanics for its fulfillment.'* This is the essence of magic.

"Fold your paper and carry it with you at all times. Focus on your star often enough to keep it emblazoned in your consciousness. Focus on it until your desires become *intentions.* An intention is much stronger than a desire. We didn't just desire to create the bodies we have today, our DNA is encoded with the absolute intention to create the bodies we have today. Once a desire becomes an intention, 90 percent of your perceived or imagined obstacles dissolve. And you have the knowledge and strength — the *will* — to deal effectively with the other 10 percent.

"Once your desires become intentions, you will create what you intend to create, no more, and no less. As James Allen wrote in *As You Think, 'You will become as great as your dominant aspiration.... If you cherish a vision, a lofty ideal in your heart, you will realize it.'*

"That's Western magic in a nutshell."

I wrote my desires at each point of my star. They came forth quickly, as fast as I could write. Each one seemed to lead to the next.

As I was writing, Bernie interrupted with an unexpected question, something no one had ever asked me, a question I hadn't ever asked myself:

"How much money do you want to make, eventually? How much money is enough?"

"That's a good question, Bernie," I said. "I have to think about that one."

"Here's the most important question: Why do you want to make money? What does it represent for you?"

The words just spilled out: "Peace and power," I said. Bernie looked highly amused.

"What do you mean?" he asked.

"A certain level of money would give me a sense of peacefulness; I'd be able to do things at my own pace, in an easy and relaxed manner — the way *you* seem to work. And it would give me the power to do what I want to do, to fulfill my purpose in life."

"Peace and power — that's good!" Bernie said. He had that delighted look again. "All right — focus on this thought, on this affirmation: *I now have peace and power.* Write it in big letters at the top of your page, above your star. Keep repeating those words: *I now have peace and power.* Keep remembering that affirmation, until your subconscious accepts it and you create it in your life.

"People don't really want *money,* they want what money can bring to them. Keep affirming you already have *peace and power* — or whatever it may be — and you'll have it!"

He laughed like a little child, utterly pleased with himself. "Got it?"

"Got it."

I drove home in a strange state — it was almost euphoria, though maybe that's too strong a word. I felt serene, completely content to be myself, doing exactly what I was doing. I drove in silence — no radio, which I almost always played as I drove.

I was perfectly content to be cruising down the road gazing silently at a world bathed in the silver light of a full moon. I was at peace.

Summary

✳ Business, like the rest of life, has a mystical and spiritual side. It used to be that science and metaphysics were considered to be almost polar opposites. But, in the twentieth century, science and metaphysics merged. Physicists tell us what the metaphysical types have been teaching for centuries: We are in reality all one, in one vast ocean of atoms, eternally interconnected with everything else in the Universe.

✳ There is nothing new in the New Age: The so-called New Age philosophy is the Perennial Philosophy that Aldous Huxley described — it's as old as humankind, and taught in Eastern traditions, Christianity, and indigenous cultures throughout the world.

✳ Eastern traditions teach about *dharma* — the importance for each of us to discover our higher purpose in life, and to realize that purpose and mission.

✳ Eastern traditions as well as Christianity teach about *karma* — all of us are rewarded with the fruits of our thoughts and actions, whether those thoughts and actions are good or bad. As you sow, so shall you reap.

✳   Indigenous peoples all over the world teach us that the earth is sacred, the earth is our Mother, and we must respect and cherish her.

✳   The Twelve Step programs have brilliant wisdom for the modern world, as well. They encourage us to keep turning our life and our will over to the care of God, as we understand God. Everyone has some conception of God, or a higher power, or the Great Mystery, or the creative force of the universe. Whenever you have a problem — business or personal — turn it over to the forces of creation, to God as you understand God. Let God work out the details. You will be shown, step by step, intuitively, what to do.

✳   All creation is magical, and we create all the time. So all of us are already magicians — though a lot of us don't know it. Visualizing your goals is an effective form of magic. Deepak Chopra wrote, "Within every desire is the seed and mechanics for its fulfillment." This is the essence of magic.

✳   As James Allen wrote, "You will become as great as your dominant aspiration. . . . If you cherish a vision, a lofty ideal in your heart, you will realize it."

KEY TWELVE

\\\\\\\//

Do what you love to do, and you'll create a visionary business, in your own absolutely unique way.

A LONG AND DIFFICULT WINTER PASSED, and I didn't hear a word from Bernie. We weathered the storms all right, though — I prayed a lot. It definitely helped: Our business stayed on course. We continued to hit our projections. There was some of Bernie's magic involved.

I made notes from everything I could remember Bernie had said, and typed them up so I could keep referring to his words and remembering them. It was far too easy to forget his words, and go back to old patterns of behavior, the old ways of thinking that focused on the problems rather than the opportunities, the ways of thinking that involved struggle and frustration and failure. But I used Bernie's magic. I carried the star that I had drawn around with me, and reflected on it now and then throughout the day. Occasionally I sat in silence and meditated on it for a while. I affirmed I had peace and power. It felt wonderful — empowering — every time I said those words to myself.

The first goal I had written on the star was the annual sales we had projected for that current year. We hit it, almost exactly — a few dollars short, but close enough for satisfaction. We had doubled the previous year's sales.

Spring finally came. It was late, and it was gorgeous — warm and sunny, with flowers blooming in so many places I had never noticed before. Bernie called one afternoon, and asked if I would like to come over. I assured him I would love to. I had no idea what to expect.

We sat on his back porch, drank coffee, and looked at the view. His yard was filled with flowers, sloping down over a hill with a view of eternity.

Someone arrived at the front door, and we got up to greet him. It turned out to be someone delivering an international feast Bernie had ordered.

Lucia joined us, her clothes speckled with dozens of colors of paint, and we had a delicious dinner of many courses.

"This is a special occasion," Bernie said. "It has been just over a year now that we've known each other. We're celebrating your year of accomplishment. To life, and to your great success."

He toasted me with his sparkling blend of fruit

juices. We joined the toast with ours.

"And to you, Bernie," I said, searching for something profound to say. I couldn't think of anything, however, so I just settled for something appropriate: "I wish you good health, happiness, prosperity, and love."

We clinked our glasses together.

"It's good to celebrate your accomplishments," Bernie said. "Take your whole crew out to dinner when you achieve your goals. And give them a nice bonus check.

"You're well on your way to success. You've got all the tools you need. Keep learning about the business, always, from everyone and everything you can. And keep re-inventing your business. It's a never-ending process. It keeps growing, organically, like every other living thing, in its own perfect way, in its own time.

"Focus on, and learn from, those who have been successful in your field. In every field, there have been great successes, and a lot of failures. Focus on the successful people. Get to know them, if you can. Read about them. Study their methods. You'll create your own methods to become successful, but never lose sight of others in the field who have already created their success.

"Celebrate their success. And learn from it."

He took a great swallow of his fruit juice, then continued.

"Celebrate the success of your competitors, too.

And even celebrate those who might think they're your enemies as well. You don't have to get down on their level; you don't have to compete with others or fight with others. You don't need any enemies. It's an abundant universe; in an abundant universe we don't have to compete with anyone for survival. There is plenty to go around. Competition — in any negative way — and animosity don't have to exist in your world. Celebrate the success of others — it'll help you create even more of your own success.

"You've got all the tools you need now. I've certainly passed on everything I can. You know how to create a vision of a business that is successful, and how to focus on that vision and manifest it, with a great deal of help from your Higher Power, or God, or the creative power of the universe, or your intuitive mind, or whatever you want to call it."

He paused, and thought for a moment.

"I just have one more thing to say to you:

"Remember what Joseph Campbell said: *Follow your bliss.'* Do what you love to do! Work with passion, live with passion, and you'll create a visionary business, in your own absolutely unique way.

"I look forward to having dinner with you again in another year — and hearing you tell me you've doubled your sales again, and are solidly profitable."

"That's my goal," I said.

"So be it, so it is," said Bernie, with surprising force.

I left not long after dinner. As I headed across the lawn toward my car, Bernie called out from the front door.

"Oh, one more thing. A little present." He disappeared back into the house and returned with a small box wrapped in shiny silver-colored paper.

I opened it right away. It was a piece of polished wood, designed to sit on a desk or table, with these words inscribed on a brass plate:

Keep away from people who try to belittle your ambitions. Small people do that, but the really great make you feel that you, too, can somehow become great.

— Mark Twain

I was touched by his gift, and by the sweet, fumbling way he gave it to me. As I started to thank him, my eyes suddenly filled with tears.

SUMMARY

✳ Keep learning about your business, always, from everyone and everything you can. And keep re-inventing your business. It is a never-ending process. It keeps growing, organically, like every other living thing.

✳ You live in an abundant universe; in an abundant universe you don't have to compete with anyone for survival. There is plenty to go around. Competition — in any negative way — and animosity don't have to exist in your world. Celebrate the success of others — it will help you create even more of your own success.

✳ Remember what Joseph Campbell said: "Follow your bliss." Do what you love to do! Work with passion, live with passion, and you'll create a visionary business, in your own absolutely unique way.

✳ "Keep away from people who try to belittle your ambitions," Mark Twain once wrote. "Small people do that, but the really great make you feel that you, too, can somehow become great."

EPILOGUE

\\|||/

The ultimate purpose of visionary
business is to transform the world
by doing what you love to do.

THE FOLLOWING PAGES *were originally in the last chapter (Chapter 12) in early drafts of this book. Several early readers of the manuscript, however, had objections to the material.*

Some readers felt the material wasn't relevant to the book; I was told the book is primarily for those who want to focus on their own business, and weren't yet ready to transform the world. Another reader said, interestingly enough, "If you leave it in there, you'll lose the East Coast." I don't know if either comment is true or not, but I ended up making a compromise that allows me to take the material out of the book and leave it in at the same time: I'm putting it in as an epilogue for you to read or to ignore, as you see fit.

I feel that the material is an important part of this book. It contains the philosophy expressed earlier in the book, but applies it in another important arena: global transformation.

We sat on Bernie's back porch, drank a blend of fruit juices, and looked at the view of the nearby flowers, the distant hills, and the eternal skies with their ever-shifting clouds.

We both sat in silence for a while, then Bernie said, "Sometimes I fantasize about writing a novel. But it's so much work to write a novel! Sometimes I ask myself, why bother?"

That was one of the very few negative things I ever heard Bernie say. It wasn't until many years later I discovered he had written several books.

"But I've got the story in my mind, and I keep adding to it, filling it out. It's a Utopian novel — there hasn't been a good Utopian novel written in years.

"It's based on the premise that, with enough money and understanding and creativity, every major problem the world now faces can be solved.

"One of the world's major problems is that it is trapped in poverty consciousness: Most people — and almost all nations, it seems — feel there really isn't enough money to go around. But, contrary to most people's beliefs, there is plenty of money: Money is infinitely available, if we know how to manifest it.

"We don't lack for money — all we lack is creativity and understanding: All we lack is *vision.*

"One person's vision can change the world — that has been proven in the past. And that's what my novel is about. Do you want to hear about it?"

"Sure!"

"It starts with a young man — or it could be a young woman, it doesn't matter. I'm not sure yet which it'll be, but it'll be a young person who creates a vital part of a new technology, builds a big business around it, and in a decade or so is worth ten billion dollars.

"He — or she — gets married to a mystical person from South America, who practices magical rituals. Together they form the most creative financial team the world has ever seen. *Every year* their assets double — in spite of the fact that they spend massive amounts of money, every year, supporting other people in becoming successful. In ten years, they are worth ten trillion dollars.

"The woman gets pregnant, and strange omens begin to happen. Flowers bloom out of season. Music is heard in the wind. An owl comes to guard their door. She has identical twins, a boy and a girl. There are miracle stories about their early years. They exhibit human and psychic powers far more quickly than any other children ever have.

"Many more brothers and sisters are born, until there are a total of twelve — six boys and six girls — and they spread over the earth, carrying the vision of their parents: a vision of a world that works.

"The children go light years beyond their parents in financial success and power to create change for the better. All the children are complete, natural masters of both fund-raising and diplomacy. They create a vast worldwide non-profit organization, dedicated to improving the quality of life for all.

"The organization is called FOCI — plural of focus — the Foundation of Creative Individuals. Its purpose is to awaken the creativity inherent in all of us, and help us all creatively solve our problems, whatever those problems may be — whether they're basic problems of food and shelter or more complex problems of education, personal growth and therapy, or fulfilling artistic or business dreams.

"The Foundation becomes the most powerful non-profit organization the world has ever imagined, more powerful than most governments. Millions of people contribute to it, because it helps so many people in so many ways.

"All over the world — eventually in some form in every populated area — Centers of Arts, Sports, and Learning are established. Simultaneously, there are massive efforts to place a safety net under the global population: to house and feed the homeless and heal the sick and addicted and support others who need it.

"The common goal is to awaken everyone's creativity: Every person in the community is invited to develop their own unique creativity, and assisted in various ways in doing so. The goal is to encourage everyone to creatively solve their problems, and then to unleash their creativity in other arenas: artistic and business and humanitarian.

"The Mother, Father, and twins become known as the Quartet, the visionary leaders of the Foundation. The Mother and Father maintain and build their private wealth, and fund the non-profit corporation that way, while the children work within the Foundation.

"Each of the twelve children is given a territory, and they leave no part of the earth uncovered. In a few short years, their impact is global.

"The Foundation of Creative Individuals empowers the individual. It is set up like Alcoholics Anonymous — no one governs anyone. The leaders are but trusted servants; they do not govern.

"FOCI of course focuses on many different things: every level of human endeavor, every level of Maslow's pyramid. Are you familiar with Maslow's pyramid of human consciousness? Those on the bottom are concerned almost entirely with food and shelter. If you don't have those things in your life, your efforts to get them are all consuming. Those a step above them are concerned with security. Those above them are free to work on their education and their personal problems, their self-esteem and psychological development. Those near the top are free to focus on their creative expression, and their fulfillment in life.

"FOCI operates on all of these levels. Those on the first levels, needing food, shelter, and security, are supported. Those who want or need emotional support can go to a wide range of free programs and support groups and varieties of therapy — everyone is encouraged to go to some kind of program, if they wish. Those who need to improve their education are supported in doing so.

"Those with creative dreams, dreams of personal fulfillment, are supported by the art and sports centers and universities and business schools. All current institutions of learning are strengthened, and many more new ones spring up everywhere.

"There's even a Bernie's School of Business, in honor of me, for dreaming all this up. It's a franchise operation, with branches all over the world, where they study my business methods, and finance thousands — *millions* — of people who go into business for themselves.

"All the art schools and business schools support and finance the dreams of those who wish to attend. Here is where a tremendous amount of energy and money is generated. Artists and businesspeople are shown how to be successful — however they wish to define success. Artists are shown how to create business plans and set up limited partnerships that finance their projects. One of the major purposes of FOCI is teaching people to write business plans, and then financing those plans, often picking up 25 to 50 percent equity in the projects. Once the artists and businesspeople are successful, they give generously back to the organization.

"FOCI donates to every genuine environmental and human rights organization. All current structures working for good are strengthened: non-profit organizations, sports centers, art centers, youth centers, child-care centers, the Guardian Angels, and so on.

"At first it works almost completely independently from any official government, but eventually it becomes a partnership with every government on earth, because all the people involved in the Foundation have enough money and power to creatively buy their way out of all of the problems of the world, and create a paradise on earth.

"They build campuses and mansions all over the world that evolve into centers of learning and diplomatic centers, where they brilliantly negotiate with local people and world leaders alike. Over a period of only twenty years, they creatively solve all the world's major problems — homelessness, starvation, war, drug abuse, violence, extinction of wildlife and plants, environmental destruction. It's all accomplished through the use of the vast sums of private wealth from the family as well as the far greater sums the non-profit businesses and fund-raising groups generate.

"Part of their magic is that nearly everywhere

FOCI invests, they eventually make profits. Those who are educated for free, for example, donate generously after they start making money. Artists and businesspeople who receive backing and guidance from the organization give back to it once they are successful. Everyone who has been helped by FOCI, or just wishes to support the goals of FOCI, is encouraged to donate 5 percent of their income to FOCI, and another 5 percent to other good causes.

"FOCI invests roughly a third of their resources into helping those at the bottom of the pyramid get food, shelter and security; a third into helping those in the middle who want education and therapy; and a third into assisting those at the top realize their dreams of business or artistic success.

"They feed the hungry, with a global network of food distribution so that there is plenty of free food for all who need it. In the process, farmers are supported as well, for FOCI buys the food at prices the farmers can live well on.

"They build shelters for the poor. They convert old military bases and old navy ships into housing, hospitals, and schools for those who need them and want them.

"They invest in the inner cities, rebuilding youth centers and schools that evolve into centers of free higher education, training people to discover their creativity and talents and ways to support themselves abundantly. What a concept! It's called a public school system.

"They buy back the rainforests and give them to the indigenous people. They educate loggers and hunters and others who are creating environmental problems, and support them until they can move into new jobs and careers that are not destructive to animals or to the environment.

"They develop solar energy, solar vehicles, clean fuels....

"They face a vast number of challenges and difficulties, of course, requiring the re-education of literally billions of people. But the single vision of the leaders is contagious, and spreads around the world.

"The movement is aided by a new generation of children, who are born with an innate sensitivity for the health of the planet. They become powerful environmentalists; the force of the children crying for change makes changes — slowly, organically — in the way things operate. I think this is now happening, and that the younger generation will make environmentally aware career choices and will have a powerful impact on all of the currently destructive businesses and individuals.

"The generation that follows that one says to their elders, 'Thanks for cleaning up the planet, but you haven't done a thing for human-rights abuses — abuses to humanity, and to all other living creatures.' And that generation creates a world in which every human being — as well as every animal, plant, and rock — is respected and cherished for its own unique creative nature, its own sacred way of being.

"They become the leaders of a new renaissance, where individual creativity flourishes, environmental balance is restored, and the world is united in peace. A revolution takes place, through natural growth and evolution, without violence.

"I'm convinced that, with enough money and vision, it could be done. And there is plenty of money out there — there is total abundance of money that can be created, without limit. So the only thing missing is the vision...."

Bernie stared into the shape-shifting clouds, intensely, wistfully. He looked the part of the visionary.

"All you need is the vision," he repeated. "Then anything is possible. I'm still working on the details.... The book has a message: The ultimate purpose of visionary business is not to make money, it is to transform the world, by doing what we love to do, and what we're here to do, whatever that is."

Bernie had once again given me plenty of food for thought. He had been so animated as he told it; the spring sun illuminated his face.

Summary

* One of the world's major problems is that it is trapped in "poverty consciousness" — most people, and almost all nations, feel there really isn't enough money to go around. But, contrary to most people's beliefs, there is plenty of money: Money is infinitely available, if we know how to manifest it.

* With enough money and understanding and creativity, every major problem the world now faces can be solved. One person's vision can change the world — that has been proven in the past.

* The ultimate purpose of visionary business is not to make money, it is to transform the world, by doing what we love to do, and what we're here to do, whatever that is.

AFTERWORD

Twenty-five Principles and Practices of Visionary Business

1. Every company needs a solid, well-written business plan that charts a clear course for the next year, and projects the vision of the business five years into the future, first in words, then in numbers. A well-written plan is your map, your visualization of the future.

2. The business plan should start with a brief, concise mission statement that is idealistic and grand.

3. Before writing the business plan, do the *"ideal scene"* process: Assume five years have passed, and your business has succeeded brilliantly, as well as you can possibly imagine: What would you like to be doing? What is your *ideal scene?* What if you could have exactly the kind of life you wanted, what would it be? Put it in writing,

and compare it with others involved in your business.

4. Plan on everything in a start-up business to take twice as long and cost twice as much as you expect. Make sure you have — or are asking for — plenty of capital, enough to cover every imaginable contingency. And add another 15 percent on top of all projected expenses for contingencies.

5. Your plan has to be strong enough to over- come every possible hurdle and obstacle, external and internal: external problems such as lack of capital, changes in the marketplace and economy, and competition, as well as your own internal obstacles of fear, doubt, lack of self-esteem or self-respect, lack of experience and knowledge. A business plan is powerful, because it sets in motion your powerful sub- conscious mind. It brings the fantasy of your "ideal scene" down into concrete terms. Once you have completed it, a vital part of your work is done: Your vision of the future has been clearly drawn. Without a vision of the future, there is no future.

6. Every successful business is based on a vision. Someone has first clearly imagined the growth and development of that business, far before that growth occurred in physical reality. Keep focused on a vision of your success, and you

will end up aligning the exact forces you need to bring about your success.

7. You have to have a higher purpose than making money in a business. When you have a higher purpose, you marshall all kinds of forces behind you that support you in your goal. Money is essential in business, but it is secondary. Each of us has a unique purpose for living, and unique talents and abilities to achieve that purpose. We should spend however much time is necessary to discover our purpose, and to live it. Then, and only then, are we fulfilled in life.

8. For every adversity there is an equal or greater benefit. That is a key to visionary business. Life is always filled with problems, but it is filled with opportunities as well.

9. There are no bad businesses, there are only poor managers. A good manager can take *any* kind of business and turn it around and make it successful. A poor manager can take any kind of business and run it into the ground. Don't dwell on pictures of failure. Keep picturing success. Spend some time in solitude, every day if you can, reviewing your goals, keeping your dreams fresh in your mind. Plan your work and work your plan.

10. Your success may take a different route than you planned. Make a clear plan, a clear path to

success, but then be flexible enough to change your plans continually as new problems and obstacles and opportunities and successes arise. Your business might look totally different in five years than you imagine it will look at this time.

11. Put the interests of the corporation before your own interests, and before the interests of any owners, any employees, or anyone else. Take care of the corporation, first and foremost, and it will take care of you, and take care of all of its owners and employees and many others as well.

12. Create an employee handbook. Include generous employee benefits: vacations, wellness days, health and dental insurance, a pension plan, and profit sharing. A substantial bonus based on profits gets everyone thinking like an owner. Give away a substantial share of your profits to your employees, and the company will do so well that, in the long run, the owners will make more than if they had kept all the profits. This is win-win profit sharing. Be sure to include every employee in the profit sharing. After several years of profits, when the company has built a substantial net worth, set up an Employee Stock Option Plan that gives a substantial part of the company to the employees. Make sure *every* employee becomes a stockholder.

13. Only you can create your success, and only you can block your success. If your visualization of success is stronger than your doubts and fears, you will succeed. When your desire becomes an *intention,* 90 percent of your perceived obstacles dissolve — and you have the inner resources to effectively handle the obstacles that remain.

14. There are two styles of management: management by crisis, and management by goals. Those caught in the management-by-crisis trap get so focused on the day-to-day problems they never have time to step back and see the big picture. Take time to support your dream with a concrete, achievable plan. Then the magic happens: All kinds of forces come into play and help you manifest your dream.

15. With ownership comes responsibility. The owners of a business have a responsibility toward the welfare of their employees and of the environment. If you can't run a business without exploiting people or polluting the planet, you should not be in that business in the first place.

16. Give a generous portion of your profits to your people and to organizations working to improve the world. If every profitable business in the world gave even just 5 percent of their profits to non-profit corporations that are

working to help people and the environment, we could end starvation around the world, house the homeless, and clean up the whole planet.

17. Money is not the final measure of a person's worth — there are far more important things: the quality of life we lead; the way we treat others, and treat our environment; the service we do for others; the amount of love and compassion we have for others; our purpose in life, and the degree to which we fulfill it; our positive contribution to others and to our planet. These things are what is truly important in life. These things are the only significant measures of a person's success.

18. It makes great business sense to follow the three rules of Pepsico's CEO: (1) love change — we either learn to love it, or resist the inevitable; (2) learn to dance — our working relationships should be a dance, not a struggle; (3) leave J. Edgar Hoover behind — hire good people, clearly define their responsibility, and let them do it their own way.

19. Hire people who are passionate about their work. Learn the difference between technicians, managers, and entrepreneurs, and hire appropriate people to do what they love to do. Treat them like adults, and they will act like adults; give them responsibility, and they will

be responsible.

20. Every business reflects the consciousness of the owner. It is extremely important to reflect on the events that have shaped our lives, and discover the core beliefs that we have created for ourselves because of those events. Once our negative beliefs are identified, they can be let go of, because they are not true — they are simply self-fulfilling; they become true if we believe them. Far better to nurture the positive beliefs that support the creative genius within each of us. You are capable of anything; there are no limits to what you can accomplish — if you believe it to be true.

21. The more you give, the more you receive — and not just financially. You receive even more important things: satisfaction, fulfillment, joy, and love.

22. The words of Christ are still brilliant today, and should be remembered: *Ask and you shall receive, seek and you shall find, knock and the door will be opened unto you. . . . Judge not, lest you be judged. . . . Love your enemies. . . . Turn the other cheek. . . . The Kingdom of Heaven is within.*

23. It's invaluable to have some kind of understanding of a higher power, to help turn life's problems into opportunities, to help you have a life well-lived. Alcoholics Anonymous sums it up simply and clearly for millions of people,

and could be helpful for millions more: *I made a decision to turn my will and my life over to the care of God, as I understand God.... I seek through prayer and meditation to improve my conscious contact with God, as I understand God, praying only for knowledge of God's will and the power to carry it out.* The most important thing for us, in order to be able to create the kind of life experience we dream of creating, is to reflect upon what we believe God to be, and to find something to turn to for guidance and inspiration. Turn everything over to God, and let God work out the details. Keep asking what God's will is, and you will be guided in your business and your life to do exactly the right thing for you.

24. Keep learning about the business, from everyone and everything you can. Keep re-inventing your business: It is a never-ending process. Celebrate your own success, and the success of others as well. Competition in any negative way and animosity don't even have to exist in your world. Follow your bliss: Do what you love to do, work with passion, live with passion, and you will create a visionary business, in your own absolutely unique way.

25. With enough money and understanding and creativity, every major problem the world now faces can be solved. And money is infinitely available, if we know how to manifest it. So all

we lack is understanding and creativity: All we lack is vision. One person's vision can change the world — that has been proven in the past. Far more than one of us are now inspiring a New Renaissance around the world, an era of peace and prosperity for all. The ultimate purpose of visionary business is not to make money, it is to transform the world, by doing what we love to do, and what we're here to do, whatever that is.

ACKNOWLEDGMENTS

\\\\\\\\\\

I WOULD LIKE TO THANK Julie Bennett, that publishing wizard (she co-published *50 Simple Things You Can Do to Save the Earth,* among other things), for reading the first draft and telling me to refocus and totally rewrite. Thanks for your honesty and insight.

I'd like to thank Kent Nerburn for reading the second draft, and giving me encouragement and insightful feedback as well. Thanks for over thirty-five pretty marvelous and remarkable years of friendship and mutual support. I am in awe of your writing ability. *Letters to My Son* is the most beautiful and profound piece of writing I've ever published. If brilliant, soulful writing determines sales, the book will sell *millions* of copies.

Thanks to Gina Misiroglu for her excellent

editing of the final draft. You are one of the finest editors I have ever worked with — sensitive, intuitive, intelligent.

Thanks to the whole team at Publishers Group West — our marketing and distribution arm — for your enthusiasm about this book. It was the people at PGW — particularly Charlie Winton, Randy Fleming, Gary Toderoff, Susan Reich, and Mark Ouimet — who felt so strongly about the book they insisted I tour nationally to support it (in *January* — thanks a lot). I appreciate your dedication and, even more, your mastery of the thankless task of distributing books throughout America and Canada. Publishers Group West is a visionary business. I wonder if Charlie Winton knew, when he started selling books out of the trunk of his car, he would one day have a company doing over a hundred million a year in sales. Somewhere along the line, he learned how to visualize very effectively.

Thanks to Auri Nogueira for her love and support, her cafe lattes and fruit juice smoothies and her passion for Brazilian dance. I know you'll succeed in your own visionary business, Wonders of Brazil. It's been fun and satisfying for me to watch a start-up business get off the ground once again and start soaring. You have all the tools you need to create complete success.

Thanks to Janet Mills for her insightful editorial ideas, and to Becky Benenate for her assistance and support far beyond the call of duty. I appreciate it immensely.

And thanks to Bernie Nemerov for believing in a naive kid, being an entertaining mentor and story-teller, and investing $80,000 in a start-up company led by someone who had absolutely no collateral and hadn't the faintest idea what a business plan or balance sheet was. This book is a tribute to you, Bernie — somehow I have the feeling you're getting a big laugh out of it, on whatever plane of existence you happen to be at the moment.

And thanks finally to a power far beyond me who is really guiding the whole show. It's a great relief to know that I'm not in charge, and all I need to do is to keep turning my problems — I mean, my challenges and opportunities — over to a higher power and listening for guidance. You've never failed me yet, and I know you never will.

Thanks to all....

SUGGESTED READING
FROM NEW WORLD LIBRARY

\\\\//

As You Think by James Allen. Written in 1904 — originally titled *As a Man Thinketh* — it is the granddaddy of New Age literature. Brief, concise, brilliant.

The Perfect Life — Ten Principles and Practices to Transform Your Life by Marc Allen. The author of *Visionary Business* shows you how to clarify what you want in life, and how to create it. This is both inspirational and practical.

Creative Visualization by Shakti Gawain. A classic, and for good reason: It shows us how, easily and effortlessly, to create what we want in life.

The Art of True Healing by Israel Regardie. Western magic in a nutshell. Contains the practices as well as the theory.

Creating Affluence by Deepak Chopra. A modern magician blends Eastern philosophy with Western science and shows us "within every desire is the seed and mechanics for its fulfillment."

The Seven Spiritual Laws of Success by Deepak Chopra. If you aren't effortlessly, joyously succeeding in life, it is simply because you have forgotten one (or more) of the Seven Spiritual Laws of Success. A brilliant work that sums it all up.

The Message of a Master — A Classic Tale of Wealth, Wisdom and the Secret of Success by John McDonald. A powerful work for the aspiring businessperson — or anyone who aspires. Written in 1934, and still visionary today.

The Instant Millionaire by Mark Fisher. A modern fable that shows us that financial prosperity and a life well lived are goals we can all achieve if we understand and practice the principles of success.

The Wonders of Solitude, edited by Dale Salwak. A collection of quotes from famous writers, spiritual leaders, and others. A book everyone in our busy, noisy world can benefit from. Truly inspiring.

Work with Passion — How to Do What You Love for a Living by Nancy Anderson. A master career consultant shows us how to do what we love for a living. This book is an entire course in fulfillment.

Prospering Woman by Ruth Ross, Ph.D. Excellent for men as well as women in enabling us to develop the power we already possess to bring the prosperity we desire into our lives. "The secret to experiencing joy in life is loving what you have while working toward what you want."

Letters to My Son by Kent Nerburn. If you are a parent, here's a beautiful collection of all the advice you would want to give to your child. Heartfelt, meaningful. The work of a great soul.

Tantra for the West — Everyday Miracles and Other Steps for Transformation by Marc Allen. A brilliant teaching from the East — tantra — brought to the West. The study of tantra shows us that every moment of our lives, rejecting nothing, is for emotional and spiritual growth. There are chapters on relationships, sex, being alone, work, money, creativity, food and drink, meditation and yoga, aging and healing, politics, enlightenment.

ABOUT THE AUTHOR

\\\\\/

MARC ALLEN is co-founder (with Shakti Gawain) and president of New World Library. He is author of several books, including *The Perfect Life — Ten Principles and Practices to Transform Your Life* and *Tantra for the West — Everyday Miracles and Other Steps for Transformation.* He is also a musician and composer, and has recorded several albums of music, including "Solo Flight," "Petals," and "Breathe." He lives in Marin County, California.

New World Library is dedicated to
publishing books and audio cassettes
that improve the quality of our lives. Our books
and tapes are available in bookstores everywhere.
For a catalog of our complete library
of fine books and cassettes, contact:

New World Library
14 Pamaron Way
Novato, CA 94949
Phone: 415 • 884-2100
Fax: 415 • 884-2199

Or call toll-free: 800 • 227-3900